This passionate, challenging and hi[...] champions the vital role of internationa[...] who give voice to 'the risky, the innova[...] marginal and the imaginative voices'.

—RICHARD SMART, Consultant for Independent Publishers Committee,
Australian Publishers Association

Susan Hawthorne's insightful and warm-hearted essay argues for a wide landscape of independent publishing to balance what is called 'mainstream', meaning the male power of big money.

—GERLINDE KOWITZKE and HILKE SCHLAEGER,
Frauenoffensive, Munich, Germany

This manifesto was written with the systemic complexity of the challenge of survival of our species in mind. Susan Hawthorne warns us brilliantly from start to finish to recognize the vital interdependence of all living systems. *Bibliodiversity* can be read as a manifesto for the defence and promotion of diversity in all its forms, but also as a master class in ethics and testimony 'to free one's self ... and not to be impeded'.

—JUAN CARLOS SÁEZ C., Director Gerente, JC Sáez Editor, Chile

In *Bibliodiversity* Susan Hawthorne explores the present and future impacts of globalization, digital publishing, censorship (including self-censorship), the declining importance of reviews, monopoly-controlled distribution systems, and social media niche market promotion. She argues for the voices of diverse and marginalised people to be heard and for fair trade and fair speech rather than free trade and free speech.

—NANCY WORCESTER, Professor Emerita, Department of Gender &
Women's Studies, University of Wisconsin, Madison, USA

This is a huge and interesting work; a precious testimony to explore and understand bibliodiversity from the point of view of a feminist publisher. Bravo!

—LAURENCE HUGUES, Directrice, Alliance internationale des éditeurs indépendants, Paris, France

Bibliodiversity should be mandatory reading for anyone within the publishing industry and core curriculum for all students of publishing to ensure sustainability for the industry. Whether you are a publisher, bookseller, librarian or writer, you are above all a reader, and you each have a responsibility to encourage bibliodiversity—start playing your role today by reading this manifesto.

—MARY MASTERS, General Manager, Small Press Network, Australia

Susan Hawthorne's ideas are brilliant. Independent publishing feeds the cultural identity of our society as well as providing a source of income and satisfaction for writers, editors, and designers. This book must be read and distributed far and wide so that everyone understands the challenges but supports the joy!

—LISA HANRAHAN, Convenor, Independent Publishers Committee, Australian Publishers Association

Photo by Renate Klein, Frankfurt Book Fair, 2013

Susan Hawthorne has worked in the book industry for more than thirty years as a writer, festival organiser, reviewer, editor, publisher and mentor. In 1991, she co-founded Spinifex Press with Renate Klein, after working as an editor for Penguin Australia for four years. She has written extensively about the industry, co-organised digital training for small and large publishers, taught Publishing Studies and Creative Writing, and has been an active member of peak bodies for publishers and writers. She is a member of the Australian Society of Authors (ASA), PEN Melbourne, Poetry Australia, Small Publishers Network (SPN) and on the Independent Publishers Committee of the Australian Publishers Association (APA). Since 2011, she has been the English-language Coordinator for the International Alliance of Independent Publishers based in Paris. She is Adjunct Professor in the Writing Program at James Cook University and Publisher at Spinifex Press.

Other books by Susan Hawthorne

non-fiction
Wild Politics: Feminism, Globalisation and Bio/diversity (2002)
The Spinifex Quiz Book (1993)

poetry
Lupa and Lamb (2014)
Valence: Considering War through Poetry and Theory (2011, chapbook)
Cow (2011)
Earth's Breath (2009)
Unsettling the Land (with Suzanne Bellamy, 2008, chapbook)
The Butterfly Effect (2005)
Bird and Other Writings on Epilepsy (1999)
The Language in My Tongue (1993)

fiction
Limen (2013, verse novel)
The Falling Woman (1992/2004)

anthologies
Horse Dreams: The Meaning of Horses in Women's Lives (with Jan Fook and
    Renate Klein, 2004)
Cat Tales: The Meaning of Cats in Women's Lives (with Jan Fook and Renate
    Klein, 2003)
September 11, 2001: Feminist Perspectives (with Bronwyn Winter, 2002)
Cyberfeminism: Connectivity, Critique and Creativity (with Renate Klein, 1999)
Car Maintenance, Explosives and Love and Other Lesbian Writings (with Cathie
    Dunsford and Susan Sayer, 1997)
Australia for Women: Travel and Culture (with Renate Klein, 1994)
Angels of Power and Other Reproductive Creations (with Renate Klein, 1991)
The Exploding Frangipani: Lesbian Writing from Australia and New Zealand
    (with Cathie Dunsford, 1990)
Moments of Desire: Sex and Sensuality by Australian Feminist Writers (with Jenny
    Pausacker, 1989)
Difference: Writings by Women (1985)

Bibliodiversity

A Manifesto for
Independent Publishing

Susan Hawthorne

First published by Spinifex Press, 2014

Spinifex Press Pty Ltd
504 Queensberry St
North Melbourne, Victoria 3051
Australia
women@spinifexpress.com.au
www.spinifexpress.com.au

Editors: Renate Klein and Pauline Hopkins
Copy editor: Maree Hawken
Cover design: Deb Snibson
Typesetting: Palmer Higgs
Typeset in Adobe Caslon and Futura
Printed by McPherson's Printing Group
Cover photograph: Estelle Disch, 'Emergence', 2014. Reproduced with permission.

National Library of Australia Cataloguing-in-Publication data:
Hawthorne, Susan, 1951–   author.
Bibliodiversity: a manifesto for independent publishing / Susan Hawthorne.
9781742199306 (paperback)
9781742199276 (ebook: epub)
9781742199252 (ebook: pdf)
9781742199269 (ebook: kindle)
Includes bibliographical references.
Publishers and publishing.
Corporations—Publishing.
Private presses.
Self-publishing.
Authors and publishers.
Books and reading—Sociological aspects.
070.5

I will go on adventuring, changing, opening my mind and my eyes, refusing to be stamped and stereotyped. The thing is to free one's self: to let it find dimensions, not to be impeded.

—Virginia Woolf, *A Writer's Diary* (1953)

CONTENTS

Introduction

The new global publishing order is the latest in a series of mergers and takeovers in publishing that have occurred over the last century. While the church quickly commandeered printing for its own purposes in the fifteenth century, many books and pamphlets were published by the cottage industry that flourished around writers and thinkers. Women and members of colonised and enslaved peoples have always encountered obstacles to getting their ideas into print but, in spite of this, marginalised groups have found ways to air their words.

During the twentieth century, the book had spread all around the world, especially the paperback with its cheap paper and floppy cover. Allen Lane, the founder of Penguin, brought this into the public domain in the 1930s. Tuppence halfpenny a copy was all he asked. I remember the rows of orange Penguins, blue Pelicans and green crime novels in our bookshop in rural Australia. The black classics had not made it there and I'd already outgrown the Puffins, but the other popular colours filled the shelves.

In the twenty-first century, we are promised that 'digital' will save us: that rock-bottom-priced eBooks are the way to go, that we can publish our own words at the click of a mouse. But how true is this? Is this the first age of mass self-publishing? Does anyone need editors? And what role can independent publishers play in a marketing-driven global economy?

The market economy, in the guise of heavily capitalised megacorporations whose names are on the lips of every reader, promises to make it all happen. The process of publishing concentration has followed the same path as the industrialisation of other products. Both seek ever-increasing control over the people whom they claim to satisfy with their products. While 'big pharma' interferes with farming methods, 'big publishing' is forever distracting us with its latest product lines, great deals, books that cost almost nothing. But like the dairy farmer who sells her milk to the supermarket below cost, the publisher is expected to sell books that have taken years of nurturing, long editing, care with the look, feel and quality of the book, for just a couple of dollars.

Independent publishers (the definitions will come later) do not pump out new titles in a factory-style process. Chances are most of the people in the production are underpaid and under-resourced but somehow they manage to produce the books anyway.

Global megacorp publishing does not encourage the quirky, the original, the risky, the inventive—the books that will become staples for the next generation because they have something new and relevant to say. Megacorp publishing is all about numbers, about sameness, about following a formula based on the latest megasuccess. Is it a J.K. Rowling lookalike story, a new erotic twist of 'seventy shades', or a twilight zone filled with zombie characters who walk like red-coated wooden soldiers? Big publishing and big bookselling with their big marketing will weed out anything different, flatten it, make it a one-size-fits-all cultural product. A line of books, like a line of lingerie. As André

Schiffrin has written of the free marketplace of ideas, it "does not refer to the market value of each idea. On the contrary, what it means is that ideas of all sorts should have a chance to be put to the public, to be expressed and argued fully" (Schiffrin, 2001 cited in Wills, 2001). In megacorp publishing each book is expected to pay for itself and all the externalities of publishing such as offices and CEO salaries. It means that books which take off slowly but have long lives, the books that change social norms, are less likely to be published.

Independent publishers are seeking another way. A way of engagement with society and methods that reflect something important about the locale or the niche they inhabit. Independent and small publishers are like rare plants that pop up among the larger growth but add something different: they feed the soil, bring colour or scent into the world.

The International Alliance of Independent Publishers defines an 'independent publisher' as one who is not in receipt of funds or support, financial or in-kind, from institutions such as political parties, religious organisations or universities, that gives them rights to make decisions on publishing. This definition does not prevent publishers from receiving grants, but the publishing program should be one that is not determined by the granting authority. Other elements of the Alliance's definition include the active participation in the running of the publishing house by those who provide the finance (e.g. it is not a short-term profit vehicle for a bank or corporation). Furthermore, that the list is one in which frontlist and backlist work in conjunction with one another. Independent publishers should ask themselves questions about their ability to promote bibliodiversity through public debate, working with independent booksellers, public libraries, and local organisations, as well as developing international partnerships with other independent publishers in producing co-editions and translations. The publishing of original work by authors is also an important element, in contrast to purchasing a sublicence for a mass-market book commodity.[1]

Independent publishers are not hybrids, they are instead the source of cultural diversity. They bring bibliodiversity to face the humungous behemoth of megapublishing and bookselling. This manifesto walks the tightrope between long-term optimism and short-term pessimism. There are many challenges for independent publishers operating in the global marketplace and the advent of digital publishing opens new opportunities while simultaneously threatening a form of recolonisation of ideas and intellectual property. Writers, publishers, booksellers, librarians, readers and reviewers operate in a politically charged environment. Publishing is a social, cultural and transformative activity, but it is also one that can be appropriated by those who are not on the side of social justice and fair speech.

---

1 The definition above is derived from a combination of discussions at meetings of the International Alliance of Independent Publishers, in particular with Spanish-language Co-ordinator, Juan Carlos Sáez, and Director, Laurence Hugues. See also Colleu (2006), pp. 94–97.

1
Bibliodiversity

> The rich countries that preach free trade apply stern
> protectionist policies against the poor countries:
> they turn everything they touch—including the
> undeveloped countries' own production—into gold
> for themselves and rubbish for others.
>
> —Eduardo Galeano, *Open Veins of Latin America*
> (1973, p. 101)

Just as biodiversity is an indicator of the health of an ecosystem, the health of an eco-social system can be found in its multiversity, and the health of the publishing industry in its bibliodiversity.

Biodiversity

Biodiversity is the complex self-sustaining system of an ecological niche in a very particular locale. It includes diversity in genetics, within species and within ecosystems. It includes plants, animals and micro-organisms. It "encompasses all of the species that currently exist on Earth, the variations that exist within species, and the interactions that exist among all organisms and their biotic and abiotic environments as well as the integrity of these interactions" (Gowdy and McDaniel, 1995, p. 182). I expand the notion of biodiversity to take in *cultural* diversity, and as the inspiration for bibliodiversity.

Multiversity

Multiversity is an epistemological approach that takes account of the location and context of the knower. It values local knowledge. It does not attempt to straitjacket those who bring the most original ideas, ideas that resist the mainstream with its global supports of religion, capital, libertarian consumerism, and militarism.

Bibliodiversity

Bibliodiversity is a complex self-sustaining system of story-telling, writing, publishing and other kinds of production of orature[2] and literature. The writers and producers are comparable to the inhabitants of an ecosystem. Bibliodiversity contributes to a thriving life of culture and a healthy eco-social system.

It is useful to think of bibliodiversity as a view from below. Like old trees in the right soil, the roots of culture are deep. Time has created a rich seam of knowledge and if a tree cannot tap into this soil of knowledge, it will die for lack of nutrients. But the tree is not alone. It is interdependent with a host of organisms and plants and animals around it.

---

2 Examples of orature include: Homer's *The Odyssey* and *The Iliad*; the Indian epic, the *Mahabharata*; Australian Aboriginal song cycles, such as *Djanggawul*; and a vast array of spoken literature from around the world. It also includes a massive range of traditional songs, poems and stories, as well as recipes for food and medicinal use. In the trades it also includes particular instructions for making objects, such as musical instruments, and more.

Just as an ecosystem is biodiverse when it has 'dynamic balance',[3] that is, when one species is not overrunning and dominating others to their exclusion, so too an eco-social system is only in dynamic balance when a host of varied voices can be heard. Homogenisation of ecosystems occurs when global farming, factory farming, agribusiness and genetically modified organisms come to dominate the environment. These are adverse effects of globalisation. Likewise in the eco-social system, the lack of media diversity and the concentration of big publishing and big bookselling reduce the possibility for a diversity of voices to be heard or read. These become 'monocultures of the mind' (Shiva, 1993) and they are just as destructive as agricultural and military monocultures. If the social habitat is overrun by epistemological monocultures—single voices all saying the same thing—there is a loss of dynamic balance and those who have something new or different to say will be ignored. In this context, the search for an approach that emphasises multiversity is the first step. In order for multiversity to thrive, an accompanying phenomenon of publishing is also required and this is where we find the need for an approach that highlights bibliodiversity.

Bibliodiversity occurs when both the deep soil of culture is nurtured and the multiplicity of epistemological stances are encouraged. I refer to this as *cultural multiversity*. Small and independent publishers contribute to the cultural multiversity through deep publishing of cultural materials (e.g. books that draw on non-homogenised cultural knowledge) as well as producing books that represent a wide range of viewpoints and epistemological positions.

---

3 For more on 'dynamic balance' see p. 38 and p. 71 below.

A group of Chilean publishers who had set up the group Asociación de Editores Independientes de Chile in the 1990s invented the word *bibliodiversidad* [bibliodiversity].

> The current financial orientation within the world of book publishing—in which large corporations with no ties to publishing are buying up publishing firms and enforcing high levels of productivity—is leading to a loss of editorial independence (International Alliance of Independent Publishers, 2007, p. 1).

Or as Françoise Benhamou said in a speech at a meeting of the International Alliance of Independent Publishers:

> In biodiversity, variety refers very simply to the number of species; in the book world, this would be the number of titles. Yet it is clearly insufficient to leave matters there. I will return to this point later. The second factor highlighted by the concept of biodiversity is balance, the balance between the species. If we look at what that means in biodiversity we see the extremely simple idea that if you have several species but some are present in huge numbers while others are very scarce, the ones with many units are likely to eat or prevail over the others. This is what is happening in the book world where it is a matter for concern that the dominance of blockbusters on supermarket shelves and, above all, in bookstore displays, is pushing out other offerings which are more difficult to promote (Benhamou, 2009, pp. 28–29).

When feminists were faced with a male-dominated international publishing industry in the 1970s and 1980s, similar challenges confronted them. The result was a coming together of publishers, booksellers and writers to share skills and engage in networking which in turn created opportunities for co-publishing.

In 1984, the First International Feminist Book Fair was held in London. This book fair brought together publishers and writers from several continents—and over the subsequent decade thousands of writers, readers, translators, publishers, booksellers, librarians and a host of others met at fairs every second year in Oslo, Montréal, Barcelona, Amsterdam and Melbourne. This was grassroots bibliodiversity. We knew that what we were doing was important, but we did not know that this thriving international network would collapse so soon. As feminist-run autonomous organisations, we had no structure, no long-term funding, and no ongoing administrative centre (ironically, many of our fairs were held in places soon to host the Olympics with its giant infrastructure).

The international feminist book fairs were possible because there was an intense upsurge of interest in feminist writing and publishing. But this too would soon be undermined by depoliticised theoretical 'positionings' as well as the development of the superstore.

The 1980s saw a gradual build-up of postmodern theory in universities. Postmodernists turned their attention on feminism, on lesbian theory and on radical class and race analyses. Soon we were hearing terms like 'gender', 'queer', 'hybridity', 'ethnicisation', instead of 'sexism' and 'misogyny', and prejudice based on sexual orientation, class and race. These new words tore the radical heart out of mass social movements. Who can attend a demonstration and yell out anything about ethnicisation? No one wants to yell about gender. What sort of slogan would 'gender-based sexual violence' make when the perfectly good word 'rape' exists? It's hatred, oppression, misogyny and exploitation that demonstrators want to make a noise about. Women call out: 'Take Back the Night', or 'Not the Church, Not the State, Women Will Decide Our Fate'; activists want to demonstrate about war, racial discrimination, poverty and destruction of the environment. Protestors want to be vocal about eugenics and discrimination based on disability or age or social exclusion. The linguistic weakening of mass social movements, the idea that your position in a society means you can't speak for anyone not the same as you, silenced millions of voices.

Postmodernism dissipated political energy (Brodribb, 1992; Bell and Klein, 1996). It took theorising out of the activist meetings into the ivory towers. Political energy was buried in some attic and left to gather dust.

The invention of the superstore was another nail in the coffin of feminist publishing. In 1993 at the American Book Expo, feminist publishers began to discuss the strategies of the superstores. Feminist booksellers had noticed that Borders was setting up across the street, around the corner or even next door to the best independent stores, many of which were feminist bookstores with a very loyal customer base. Borders immediately ordered the same key stock for their stores but they could sell books more cheaply and also offer coffee and snacks, and before long feminist writers were being asked to speak at events at superstores. It's not hard to conclude that the 'loyal' customers were soon visiting these stores instead. Remember that women generally have less disposable income than men, so the appeal to cheapness worked alongside all the other niceties. You might think that, even if the feminist bookstores didn't make it, this situation would be good for the feminist publishers of those books with double the number of outlets available. Initially it was. But feminist publishers found themselves with insufficient stock and consequently ordering reprints (in this period a reprint would need to be a minimum run of 1,500–2,000 copies to keep the unit cost low enough). Having arranged a reprint they sometimes found that Borders had over-ordered stock and was now returning massive numbers of books, leaving the publisher with far too many books and increased warehouse bills. It was also soon the case that when the original independent feminist bookstore folded due to lack of customers, the superstores no longer ordered the core stock that had been held by the feminist bookstore. They certainly held none of the more obscure titles which found customers in the feminist bookstore. Indeed, many of those titles were not ordered by the superstores or, if they were, would be difficult to find in the overstocked stores with their less precise categories. Both bookstores and publishers struggled to survive. This coincided with two other developments.

The technologisation of the book industry was just beginning. Borders and other superstores had the financial resources to computerise all stock in their retail outlets. The lower turnover independent stores relied on knowledgeable staff who knew their stock and who could take a customer to the correct shelf in the shop. Most of the independent booksellers had neither the knowledge base for technology, nor the finances to move into this new way of operating. And even those who did, rarely survived. The other element was the establishment of amazon.com. This was a direct attack on one of the most established feminist retailers, Amazon Bookstore in Sacramento. The proprietors of this store protested. They took amazon.com to court. They won a payout, but they still lost because they could no longer stay in business. When other store owners saw this outcome, many lost heart and gave up struggling to survive.

By the end of the 1990s, few feminist bookstores remained. Only those with good marketing skills, the resources in knowledge and money to move into the era of computerised inventory, and a solid customer base which understood the politics of survival, continued to exist. The first impact was felt in North America with feminist stores in Canada and the USA succumbing, while feminist publishers followed suit leaving only a handful. Booksellers and publishers in other parts of the English-language world were also soon affected as globalisation spread and superstores were established in other territories.

Feminist publishers were the canary in the mine. Other publishers are now feeling a similar pinch. An American editor, in an interview with Gisèle Shapiro in 2007, commented on the difficulty of getting translated books into large chains:

> Because the big chain, when we arrive with these fictions in translation, they now have what is called a 'skip', which means that for instance there is a [chain] which has 1,200 bookstores they take zero, not one available copy among books in translation (Shapiro, 2014, p. 39).

This scenario reflects, in the publishing industry, what had been going on in the manufacturing and agricultural industries for some time. This is well documented elsewhere (Hawthorne, 2002). What is not, is that another parallel industry was in a period of massive expansion. It too was assisted by the new technology of the Internet,[4] new rules on global trade and the postmodern theoretical coup in universities and governance institutions, such as national governments, but also supragovernmental organisations, such as the International Labour Organization (ILO) and the United Nations (UN). This was the sex industry: pornography and prostitution, which also included the trafficking of women's bodies as well as body parts (surrogacy and organ trafficking).[5]

I make this link because the two—the advent of the Internet and increased commodification of women's bodies through prostitution—are not unrelated (Bell, 2001). The demise of the spread of ideas is always connected to new forms of oppression. As centres for feminist ideas disappeared, the rise in a libertarian ideology of individual consumerist 'choice' came into prominence. Instead of centres of activism, many feminists were directed to put their energies into non-government organisations (NGOs) which were dependent on funding from governments or corporations and therefore were often too compromised in their objectives. A few, who understood the underlying political agenda, managed to continue with their original objectives. What became critical to their survival was independence from institutions, including governments, universities, and large corporations, especially those with shareholder-driven decision making. The disaster of

---

4 I first experienced the power of the Internet in Bangladesh in 1993, at a conference organised by Farida Akhter of the research and activist NGO, UBINIG. It was clear from the start that as feminists in Australia and Bangladesh, we needed this means of communication. We were already sharing information internationally via fax, mail and through meetings. The slowest places to take up email were those who considered they were at the centre of the world.

5 For a feminist analysis of these subjects see Ekis Ekman (2013), Raymond (1994), and Raymond (2013).

'bathplug publishing'—where books are more or less the same product in different colours—was exemplified in Australia when REDGroup, a corporate entity made up of Borders, Whitcoulls and Angus & Robertson, owned by Pacific Equity Partners, went into voluntary liquidation in February 2011. A combination of the high debt-burden policies of private equity groups plus errors of judgement regarding eBook retailing (Lim, 2011) meant that corporate memory was fragmented, lost and not replaced. Bookselling in the hands of large corporations means that all the bookshops sell the same stock from stores that look the same. It might be a windfall for some mainstream publishers with big marketing budgets, and the occasional quirky book from the margins, but it is not a model that is useful for local communities with particular interests and needs.

In the same period as superstores were entering the landscape of publishing, moves were being made on writers. In the USA, where the film industry has a lot of clout, scriptwriters would be commissioned and paid a flat fee for a film script. The studios contracted the assignment of copyright to the producers. Writers in this market lost their copyright for a fee. Universities, academic journals and presses soon followed suit. They argued that writers were already being paid for their writing through academic salaries, so universities could claim copyright on the basis that it was done as part of the writer's employment. And journals and academic publishers argued that writers did not need the income and their work would not be published otherwise. In an environment of publish-or-perish, academics needed refereed publications for promotion and tenure.

The academic environment has shifted once again and there are good reasons to argue against these conventions.

Assignment of copyright remains an unethical provision when academics do not have security of tenure. This is more and more the case as academics work on a sessional basis. Many ongoing contracts have provision for a summer recess, meaning that the job is active for only nine to ten months of the year. Salaries for such positions are lower, and courses can be cut without notice, leaving the academic without paid work.

There has been an explosion of creative industry courses in recent decades. Not only art and music schools, as in the past, but degrees in creative writing, design, poetry, theatre, circus arts and more are filling university quotas. If a poem is written during working hours or during a sessional contract, is it reasonable that the university should claim copyright? Poets are perhaps the worst paid of all creative artists, so it is not equitable that a poem should be treated in the same way as a patent for a scientific invention made on a tenured university position. The copyright law is framed around the scientific breakthrough—'the top end of town', if you like. But the poet is treated as if her or his poem will go on earning millions of dollars for the next seventy years. This sounds foolish, but it is what some publishers are asking of authors when a contract includes the words 'assignment of copyright' and that copyright is extended to the institution.

No publisher needs copyright assigned to them. All they need is an exclusive licence. The only thing that this changes is what happens after the death of the author. Assigned copyright remains in the hands of the film studio, university, academic journal or press. The standard term of copyright in the USA, Europe and Australia is the life of the author plus seventy years.[6] Who is around to take advantage? Very few small and independent publishers will be, since the vast majority of these depend on the energy and vision of the founders. By contrast, institutions—film studios, universities and journals—will still exist.

A further right important in publishing is 'moral right' which entails three separate rights that can only be exercised by individuals. It includes the right to be attributed, the right not to be falsely attributed, and the right to integrity which prohibits derogatory treatment which would be harmful to the author's reputation (ComLaw, 2000). Moral right is particularly important for those who resist the status quo. Feminists, activists against racism and environmentalists not infrequently see their words distorted and misrepresented. This is an infringement of the author's moral right. For example, if an anti-forest-industry song were to be used to promote clear-felling in World Heritage areas, that would constitute an infringement of the integrity of authorship. The other aspect is correct and prominent attribution with the correlative that one should avoid false attribution. Given that writers outside the mainstream are frequently the originators of new ideas and new ways of expressing those ideas, assertion of moral right is important for independent publishers to acknowledge on behalf of authors.

---

6 The exceptions are for government, where the period is first publication plus fifty years, and anonymous (say, company publications without an individual author named) where it's first publication plus seventy years.

2
One size fits all

> Ultimately I did convince the editors that mention
> of my race was central to the whole sense of the
> subsequent text; that my story became one of
> extreme paranoia without the information that I am
> black; or that it became one in which the reader
> had to fill in the gap by assumption, presumption,
> prejudgment, or prejudice. What was most
> interesting to me in this experience was how the
> blind application of principles of neutrality,
> through the device of omission, acted either to make
> me look crazy or to make the reader participate
> in old habits of cultural bias.
>
> —Patricia J. Williams, *The Alchemy of Race and Rights*
> (1991, p. 48)

In the move to globalise publishing and the distribution of books, the desire to homogenise is apparent. Outside the global industry are independent booksellers and publishers who operate differently. Each is sensitive to the local environment and knowledgeable about local social, political, and cultural issues. A bookstore in an inner city area has a different clientele than one in a suburban or rural setting. Likewise, a bookshop serving a large multicultural or particular social group will stock titles to satisfy that local need. A superstore will, by and large, hold inventory across its stores that is pretty much the same. They will order eccentric stock for customers but are unlikely to respond to local needs. An additional problem is the creation of a 'monopsony', where the buyer has such a powerful grasp on the market that it can force prices down (the opposite of a monopoly, where a single seller can force prices up). The result is false savings for consumers because publishers will cease to exist if a large percentage of their output is not economically viable.

It is easy to see how bibliodiversity reflects biodiversity.

The ecological environment that is biodiverse responds to the local conditions of rainfall, soil type, temperature, wind factors and the like. An ecological environment in which external inputs are pretty much the same (for example, instead of working with the local rainfall crops are irrigated, or they are fertilised to some average soil type, or pesticides are used) will produce homogenised crops which take little effort to sell in the global market (because the same marketing can be used for the homogenised commodity). The multinationals and free-traders argue that the overall quality is more consistent so retailers and customers know what they are getting. In their marketing they minimise the adverse effects of pesticides, genetically modified organisms (GMOs) and other unnecessary inputs. They claim that the products are cheaper. They never factor in the long-term impacts of externalities which could include cancer, compromised immune systems, and increased allergic reactions. In the meantime, they fund their own research to show just how beneficent their every move is.

Global publishing operates on the same basis. Books that do not threaten the status quo, that do not question either

politically or imaginatively, the mainstream view, are published
in enormous numbers. They sit in oversupplied piles at the front
of retail outlets (often barely recognisable as bookshops). They
offer themselves as '3 for the price of 2', or at discount, or in
large formats that use more resources (publishing's externalities)
to print and distribute. A few authors receive large advances, and
the incomes of others not in that category shrivel. These large
advances are another kind of externality because they come with
huge marketing budgets, overseas travel and the stellar marketing
accompaniments of hotel chains, superstores, airlines, even wine
and catering services.

Homogenisation of publishing produces a few star authors,
most of whom write about a distorted and popularised version of
a ten- or twenty- or fifty-year-old idea, but the idea is watered
down, made palatable for the generalised taste of the uninformed
reader. These ideas are then sold as if they had some resemblance
to the original idea. Sometimes they are simply badly done;
other times they are poisonous, distorting the ideas to such an
extent that the originators shudder each time their words are
repeated in unrecognisable contexts. As if the bright red but
tasteless supermarket tomato were the juicy, fruity sweet and
sharp tomato of the home garden of fifty years ago. Gradually,
customers' expectations are changed. Readers stop demanding
well-edited, thoughtfully argued, imaginatively structured books.
Instead, they get abstruse, murky, mistake-ridden texts that are
meaningless and inaccessible. At the other end of the market are
books that are clichéd, shallow, predictable and simplistic. What
a great time to give up reading, turn on your computer, your TV,
your tablet, your phone or whatever the latest electronic device

is, and lose yourself in the mayhem of pornography, sport, kitten videos or ever more time-consuming online social friendship circles.

When Don Watson (2003) wrote *Death Sentence: The Decay of Public Language*, he missed the deathly word 'gender', though he included terms like 'empower', and 'outcome'. Even his later work, *Dictionary of Weasel Words* (2005), with longer lists, still failed to include the word 'gender'. He missed it because men know that gender does not apply to them. Likewise, white people know that racism is something they can ignore, and the upper classes are forever complaining that the working class and the poor only have themselves to blame for their predicament, or that class is a result of 'choices' people have made.

But racism and poverty are *real* human situations. Most of those bearing the brunt of racism belong to groups of people whose land has been stolen, whose livelihoods were shifted from autonomous self-sustaining activities to ones dependent on the coloniser, the slave owner, the pimp, the corporate boss or the 'top dog' criminal running a protection racket.

Likewise, misogyny is also real. It results in the murder, rape and beating of millions of women each year. This is not about 'gender', but about women as a sex-class. The vast majority of the world's poor are women. As geographer, Joni Seager, concludes: "Women constitute the single biggest group of the poor. They are among the poorest of the poor" (1997, p. 121).

If progressive social movements took this fact seriously there would need to be a substantive rethinking of policies, and the objectives of those policies. It's a truism that if the poorest and most dispossessed cease to be poor and dispossessed, then everyone's life could be considered reasonably good. A few of the super-rich or over-endowed might not have as much money, but since it was excess baggage it will be barely missed. And the lack of money will not be life threatening; indeed, it might well improve the lives of the bored and cynical billionaires who no longer know what to do with themselves in their over-stimulated and often drugged-out states.

Misogyny and racism are both important to strongly oppose. Women are under constant attack from those who create sexualised images, from threats of violence, and from actual violence, whether it be the 'corrective rape' of lesbians, sexual abuse of girls and boys, or the violence of shared photos and videos online and over mobile devices. 'Conventional' violence against women in the home, on the street and in the workplace continues as new forms are found: 'lingerie football', homogenised brothels, trafficking of women across borders and within states.

The practice of homogenisation similarly structurally underpins the ideology of racism. The othering of the unknown. The powerful, in their own sense of entitlement, have great trouble in recognising their inability to empathise with anyone who does not share the same kinds of entitlements.

> Racism can be reduced neither to racist theory, nor to racist practice. Theory and practice do not cover the whole field of racism, which extends beyond conscious thought. As an ideology racism is opaque, unconscious of its own meaning (Guillaumin, 1995, p. 29).

The racist does not consider the concept of 'whiteness' (Morrison, 1993, pp. 9–10) as problematic, only other skin colours or features associated with a hated group. It is a matter of marking the body of the other. In the case of racism this occurs primarily through skin colour, but it can take the form of dressing practices or marks on the body (tattoos, hairstyles, facial and bodily ornamentation). In the world of the racist, the 'unmarked' body is 'white'. Such 'marking' is extended to other groups, each in turn highlighting a difference from the entitled, unmarked body. The marked body is extended to women (Hawthorne, 2002), the crippled (Mairs, 1992), the mad (Jeffs, 2000), the unpredictable (Hawthorne, 1996); and just like racist ideology, to discourses of heterosexuality (Wittig, 1992, p. 25). Challenging the ideas of the 'entitled' is central to the concept of publishing bibliodiversity. Publishers who take up the intention to contribute to bibliodiversity challenge stereotypes that sometimes attach to 'publishing sensations'. Success in the margins can mean that an author is pigeonholed as 'exotic', a 'rabid feminist' or the voice of the traumatised or sexually defiant. These then become the fulcrum of new stereotypes. Publishers who simply follow the latest publishing successes might as well be producing bathplugs of different colours. It is the opposite of publishing for bibliodiversity.

3
The soil

> I have doubled in age and am learning
> the internal properties of cow
> *stand your ground* calls my father
> as the biggest cow of the herd
> breaks away and runs straight at me
> I wave my arms about wave the stick at the end of my arm
> she is still running
> I jump and scream and wave
> two metres before I am history
> she veers sideways and returns to the herd
>
> I have found my cow inside
> I have learnt the internal property
> that she will give way if you stand your ground
> *stand your ground* I say to myself
> even the internal cow is impressed
>
> —Susan Hawthorne, *Cow* (2013, p. 2)

I grew up in rural Australia. I was lucky to be brought up in a household that had books and where reading and storytelling were encouraged. We did not have easy access to libraries, and TV did not materialise until after my childhood was over. We did have a local picture theatre that we attended at least once, sometimes twice, a week. I used to think that being a country girl from Australia was a disadvantage. But that rural knowledge which I had thought disadvantaged me, in the long term, I have come to see as the most valuable heritage I have.

Out of this background I have become a writer and a publisher. I inherited a love of books from my mother and a love for storytelling from my grandmother. I have belonged to many marginal knowledge systems during my life and when I first entered publishing I remembered the advice of Valerie Solanas (1967) who implored women not to be one of the "approval-seeking Daddy's Girls" (p. 41) but to "become members of the un-work force" (p. 42) and change the system.

The other important element of my childhood was nature. Growing up on a farm, with native bushland as our playground, I developed a profound connection with the natural world that can't be entirely expressed in words. My parents had an intuitive sense of ecology; they cared about trees, about the need for shade for sheep. And although they used the technologies of their time, pesticides and fertilisers, they were never careless, and it was my mother who first mentioned the name Rachel Carson to me. In *Silent Spring* (1962), Carson uncovered the damage to the environment caused by DDT and other pesticides. As a farming woman and an intellectual, my mother was shaken by *Silent Spring*. I was too young to know what they had done previously, but after reading this book, my parents took greater care, and though they continued to use pesticides they did so sparingly. They ensured that we children were never around at these times, and my father wore protective gear.

So what's the point of all this autobiography? It is that the personal is political. The soil is the basis of ecology. The wild seed will affect biodiversity and the creative wild type will contribute to the health of the culture. Bibliodiversity is the production of local and marginal knowledges outside the mainstream. The producers of bibliodiversity inhabit the margins: socially, politically and often geographically and linguistically (Ndumbe, 2007; Bell, 1998/2014).

4
Multiversity

Ethnocentrism is the tyranny of Western aesthetics.

—Gloria Anzaldúa, *Borderlands / La Frontera*
(1987, p. 68)

The concept of 'multiversity'[7] is one that has, at its centre, respect for systems of knowledge born out of experience as well as through research and study. Interactions between different knowledge systems are important in the development of systems which value the collective whole, the self-sustaining organism, the consequences and the contexts. Ugandan Paul Wangoola (2000) has also proposed a multiversity.[8] For him, multiversity is a challenge to the ways in which knowledge is structured in Western systems, in particular in universities where abstraction and disconnection from place result in specialist discourses that cannot communicate with one another across disciplines. He proposes a Mpambo Multiversity which actively resists modernisation and its accompanying "[d]isconnects from culture" (pp. 270–272).

---

7   It is interesting to note the relationship of the word 'university' to the word 'universal'.

8   I thought I had invented the term 'multiversity' around about the year 2000, but discovered in 2001 that Paul Wangoola had also used it. His use, as a different kind of university, is the more usual application of the term. The concept of a multiverse goes back many thousands of years in Hindu cosmology.

The guiding principle behind Mpambo is that being rooted in their own knowledge bases people can engage in dialogue, synthesis, articulation, partnership, collaboration, the building of synergies and cross-fertilisation: all of this across sectors, knowledges, cultures and civilisations (p. 274).

'Marginal knowledges' have contributed significantly to feminist knowledge. The 'multiversalist', in contrast to the 'universalist', recognises that universals tend to work against the most dispossessed members of society since they deny the worth of the knowledge of the dispossessed. The multiversalist, by contrast, recognises that there are many different ways of organising knowledge, and that those who live close to the biophysical world have the best knowledge of, and are well-versed in, the local conditions; likewise, that the poor, women, and people marginalised for a multiplicity of reasons have a great deal to offer with their perceptions and understanding of the world. Wangoola explains the name:

After the harvest the mother selects the best seeds for careful and safe keeping for planting the next season. Thereafter permission is given to eat the rest. In the Lusoga language of Uganda mpambo means the best of the seeds that are kept away for propagation (p. 277).

The multiversalist recognises a world in which existence of a multiplicity of alternative knowledge forms is important to human knowledge as a whole (p. 273). The caution here is that respect for the way in which knowledge forms are structured is important, and appropriation or commercialisation of such knowledge results in their distortion. For, just as money in Indigenous Warlpiri society in Australia transforms social meaning (Bell, 1983/2002), so does the commercialisation of ideas which are structurally anathema to an economy not based on money.

Appropriation is central to the methodology of capitalism. It works by an institution (media outlet, university, publishing company, NGO, corporation or foundation) taking an idea put forward by some person or group at the edge of the public intellectual sphere. This idea is then distorted, so that it contains some of the words, but the concepts are twisted and used in ways unintended by its originators; that is, it breaks the originators' moral rights. Next, this distorted form is 'sold back' to those who were not part of the idea generators, but perhaps to the side or following in the next generation. This idea is then taken up, glamourised, given lots of media, festivals, and educational space. Those who created the original idea are ignored or vilified by the latest users of the idea because by now, the originators are told they are wrong.

In recent years there has been a spate of workers wearing fluorescent vests and hard hats. The wearing of such clothing was originally a health and safety issue for those working in dangerous places, such as roads, on some machinery in factories, or similar places where visibility was important. In February 2014, the CEO of the Ford plant at Geelong (Australia) was speaking on TV wearing his fluoro outfit; politicians frequently don them for greater media visibility. It is an appropriation of the idea of the working class. If the CEO looks the same, maybe he's really a good guy. One of us!

Similar appropriations are made by environmental sceptics who frame their anti-environmental message in a cloak of fighting poverty and hunger. One very fine example is the line that genetically modified (GM) foods will solve world hunger. This is false marketing and not supported by the evidence (e.g. Crouch, 2001; Schmitz, 2001; Shiva, 2012; Hawthorne, 2002). The so-called green revolution, whose purveyors claimed they would bring agricultural prosperity to India, has turned out to be an agricultural disaster. Vandana Shiva points out "how contemporary scientific enterprise is politically and socially created and ... absolves itself from all responsibility for failures" (1991, p. 23). She goes on to argue that the Punjab, where so much effort was put into creating a 'green revolution', has become "a region riddled with discontent and violence. Instead of abundance, Punjab has been left with diseased soils, pest-infested crops, waterlogged deserts and indebted and discontented farmers" (p. 19). In agribusiness and the pharmaceuticals industry every failure is a new business opportunity (Hawthorne, 2003b).

In the feminist movement, the biggest appropriation has been the turning of prostitution into 'sex work' by pimps, sex buyers and apologists for the sex industry who claim to speak for 'feminists'. This appropriation ensures that women are kept 'in the horizontal position',[9] that women are exploited, expected to put up with violence, and pretend to enjoy pornographic displays in which they are harmed and brutalised.[10]

---

9 In 1964, Stokely Carmichael said: "What is the position of women in SNCC? The position of women in SNCC is prone" (Hayden and King, 1965). SNCC was the Student Nonviolent Coordinating Committee. From direct recollections of a member of the SNCC known to me, it caused many women to leave the organisation which they had worked hard to support.

10 For further reading see Raymond (2013); Sullivan (2007); Ekis Ekman (2013); Tankard Reist and Bray (2011); Dines (2010); Jeffreys (1997); Bray (2013); Stark and Whisnant (2004).

The publishing industry often participates in these appropriations which lead to the decimation of independent publishers who publish to movements and for movements. Superstore booksellers were instrumental in the decimation of feminist publishing. Will eBooks be the method used to kill ecological publishing?

5
Production

Bibliodiversity appears today to be threatened by an
editorial glut and financial concentration in the world
of publishing, which paves the way to the supremacy
of a handful of major publishing groups and the
quest for high productivity.

—International Alliance of Independent Publishers,
'Bibliodiversity' (2014a)

In *Close to Home*, Vandana Shiva introduces the concept of
creation and production boundaries (1994, pp. 140–141). In the
world of farming, home gardens and animals whose milk or eggs
are harvested for home use would fall outside the production
boundary. In the world of books, a self-published text would fall
outside the production boundary. Such works do not count as
part of the countable economy because they are produced for
private use (profit is not their primary cause for existence) or
for domestic or altruistic consumption. In the counting of gross
domestic products (GDPs) such creation is economic suicide.
But let us think for a moment of some historical examples.

Virginia Woolf was published by the Hogarth Press, a
press run by Leonard and Virginia Woolf. She did a great deal
of the typesetting and packaging of books. Shakespeare and
Company, a Paris-based bookshop run by Sylvia Beach and
Adrienne Monnier, published James Joyce's *Ulysses* (1918).

Bryher (Winifred Ellerman) privately published the work of American poet, HD (Hilda Doolittle). I mention these three modernists because they now have significant literary industries that have grown around their work. Under the commercial model of publishing, very little of their work would ever have been published because they were all breaking new ground, experimenting, or writing in ways that simply were not popular at the time. They all contributed the equivalent of an ecological boost to the culture that is bibliodiversity. When Virginia Woolf set type for the Hogarth Press, this was an art form several hundred years old and required her to become a type compositor. Woolf was engaged in taking over the means of production and today would be seen as a self-published writer. Long before the mass rise of self-publishing, Virginia Woolf reflected on the benefit of being on the inside of this process, namely, that you are not beholden to the quirks of fate and fashion that can make or break a writer. Indeed, Woolf said of herself that she was "the only woman in England free to write what I like" (Woolf, 1953/1975, p. 83).

Eleanor Catton, the author of *The Luminaries* (2013a), reaffirms the importance of literature as more than just consumerism.

At its best, literature is pure encounter: it resists consumption because it cannot be used up and it cannot expire. The bonds that are formed between readers and writers, between readers and characters, and between readers and ideas, are meaningful in a way that the bonds formed between consumers and products can never be. Literature demands curiosity, empathy, wonder, imagination, trust, the suspension of cynicism, and the eradication of prejudice; in return, it affords the reader curiosity, empathy, wonder, imagination, trust, the suspension of cynicism, and the eradication of prejudice (Catton, 2013b).

Bibliodiversity, like biodiversity, is not just about profits. It is about creating a long-lasting and sustaining literary culture. Literature and orature create culture and are the basis of films, theatre, music, art and many other cultural forms. Imagine a world without fairy stories, poetry, songs and all the art forms that allude to the tales that humans have told over many millennia.

In writing about biodiversity, Timothy Swanson points out:

> Biodiversity serves a distinct function within the R&D process. It acts as a source of new stocks of information which can then serve as the base from which to develop new innovations. Once brought within the process it is assimilated bit by bit into the commercial sector and investigated as such (1996, p. 6).

Mainstream publishing is equally dependent on independents for cultural R&D. One of the problems independent publishers face is how to keep cultures alive without committing the sin of assimilation.[11] How can we do this? Importantly, it takes a clear intention to refuse to assimilate; for example, to resist the temptation to make the language more 'acceptable' for mainstream readers. In Australia, this is an important aspect in working with Indigenous writers since Australian English and

---

11 The word 'assimilation' has different cultural overtones in English and French. In English, used in relation to cultural assimilation, it means that a person from outside Australia should take on the social norms, the language and the habits of 'Australians' (and it is not Aboriginal Australians who are the signified group). In French, 'assimilate' means to digest something, to break it down, its original form gone; and you can't tell the cheese from the potato.

Aboriginal English are not identical. Likewise, as Australian publishers we have battled to maintain our Australianness, along with Australian spelling, when selling rights to UK or US publishers.

The European colonial languages—English, French, German, Dutch, Spanish and Portuguese—have a range of diaspora languages across the colonised world. Publishers in these former colonies are constantly pushing back against what is standard and what is not. Furthermore, the original languages of the colonised countries have, in many instances, been annihilated (this is the case with the vast majority of Australia's Indigenous languages). Where languages do survive, those publishing in 'language' find they are trumped by the dominant language. In Europe itself, the Basque publishing house Txalapata has managed to survive for fifty years by creating a book club. Some Spanish booksellers will not stock Txalapata's books because they say they consider Txalapata to be terrorists (Soto, 2013). It doesn't take being called 'terrorist' to make books invisible or difficult to obtain. Finding books in African languages, even in Africa, is a challenge, and the same can be said for indigenous and colonised languages everywhere.

Feminist writers have faced similar challenges and have to fight to keep feminist language and concepts alive in the face of media and mainstream backlash, appropriation and distortion (Hawthorne, 2004; 2012a). These are all battles against assimilationist homogenisation.[12]

---

12 For a longer discussion of knowledges and cultural homogeneity see Hawthorne (2002, pp. 86–109). For a critique of assimilationist policies see Hawthorne (2004).

6
Feminism

> If we comply, we signal our docility and our
> acquiescence in our situation. We need not, then,
> be taken notice of. We acquiesce in being made
> invisible, in our occupying no space. We participate
> in our own erasure.
>
> —Marilyn Frye, 'Oppression' in *The Politics of Reality*
> (1983, p. 2)

An essential element in bibliodiversity is feminism. Feminism is the recognition that women are oppressed and discriminated against in the global context. It is not sufficient, however, simply to acknowledge this oppression. An indispensable part of feminism is doing something to change that situation.

Women's poverty, as Seager (1997) indicates, is replicated in societies around the world. Women's poverty is also reflected in the absence of power to speak freely and, along with this, for their speech to be heard.

Feminism brings new insights to poverty, to questions of power and its use in society. It brings significant questions for men who continue to behave in such a way as to maintain the social norm that would be loudly criticised if it were not ingrained, garden-variety misogyny. In other words, corporate treatment of workers or peasants, or the treatment of one caste by another, or the treatment of a particular cultural or ethnic group, is resoundingly analysed and criticised as oppression, as hate speech, and recognised as politically and socially unacceptable.[13] When the same violations are committed against women they are widely ignored.

Romantic love is implicated in women's oppression (Greer, 1971; Firestone, 1971; Wittig, 1976) because women are the only oppressed class who are *expected* to love their oppressors. And while there are instances of the slave loving his/her slave owner, and the hostage loving their kidnapper, what is clear in the oppression of women is that this state is normalised. This is typified in the phenomenon of Stockholm Syndrome,[14] in which women obey and even adore the men who have kidnapped them. That women should adore while men become the patrollers of hostage women, is barely noticed when it surfaces in the ordinary lives of ordinary women and men (Graham, Rawlings and Rigsby, 1994). As Lara Fergus (2005) has perceptively suggested, women are given 'temporary protection visas' in men's households.

Under such regimes, women—that is, billions of people on this earth—are represented as a homogenised group, all of whom are looking for just one thing: a man. Men's media, the advertising industry, the political machinery, the educational sector, toy manufacturers, sporting companies, the pharmaceutical industry and the sex industry, just to name a few, emphasise women's bodies, self-perception, and sexual availability—for men.

---

13 The names Fanon (1973), Said (1995), Asante (1999) are well-known, while the names Mies (1986/1999), Anzaldúa (1987), Tuhiwai Smith (1999) are known mainly in their respective areas of specialty, namely: colonisation and feminism, lesbian scholarship or queer theory, and Indigenous studies. What they share is a focus on women's lives.

14 First identified by Judith Herman (1992).

Against this juggernaut, feminists are derided as man-haters, in a Dalyesque manoeuvre of reversal (Daly, 1978) which once again blames women for all the ills of the planet. But to return to the issue of women's poverty: how is it possible for the poorest of the poor to be responsible for the world's wars, for the rape and torture of millions of people, for the agricultural and ecological destruction of the earth, for the pollution of earth, seas, skies and even space, for the rapid extinction of animals and plants, for climate change? These poorest of the poor simply do not have the resources to do any of these things. Indeed, research shows that when women have money they tend to spend it on survival items, such as food, shelter, medicines and education for their children and other members of their family (however that is constituted); men, on the other hand tend to spend on individual luxury items for their own consumption: alcohol, tobacco, petrol, drugs, gambling and prostitutes (Hynes, 1999).

It looks as if there has been a concerted marketing campaign against feminists by those who do have the resources and the distributive power of technology.

7
Pornography

> They made it clear from the start that the slightest
> deviation from the norm would be punished. They
> turned everything into prisons, even our own bodies.
>
> —Abigail Bray, *Misogyny Re-Loaded* (2013, p. 1)

A test case for those interested in bibliodiversity is that of
pornography. A number of small and independent presses in
different countries have resorted to publishing pornography in
order to survive. They justify it on the grounds that it gives them
the cash flow to publish other interesting books.

What does pornography do? And to whom does it do that
something? Pornography demeans the person at the other end
of the camera whose image is then published conventionally or
electronically. That person is expected to put up with humiliation, pain, degradation and dehumanisation. That person is
expected to accept being portrayed as dirty, as filth, as nothing
more than a hole, and as a slave. That person is almost always a
woman. Pornography treats all women as if they were the same;
it homogenises women and makes of women a group to be
exploited and put down in all the same repetitive, boring ways.

Who profits from pornography? Capitalists, companies and
individuals after fast money, corporations with massive publicity
budgets. As Gail Dines reports, in 2006 the global pornography
industry was worth US$96 billion, and in the USA alone,
$13 billion (2010, p. 47). The market is growing significantly

every year and now, eight years later, it will be worth even more. At the individual end, men benefit because they gain a sense of power or a sense of camaraderie with their peers (Stark and Whisnant, 2004).

What kind of social system allows one group (women) to be so exploited by another (men) and still have supporters among progressives who think that porn is 'just good fun' and helps us keep our publishing houses alive?

Neither pornography nor racism nor any other kind of institutionalised hatred can be part of a bibliodiverse publishing industry. Treating women as a monoculture to be harvested does not contribute to bibliodiversity. Just as slavery demeans both slave and slave owner, pornography and prostitution operate in a similar way (Tankard Reist and Bray, 2011; Cacho, 2012).

Bibliodiversity is based on respect for others, on dynamic balance in society, and on a rejection of monocultures. Pornography, racism, sexism, homophobia, as well as discrimination based on religion, ethnicity, dis/ability, age, caste, class and sexuality, all spring from disrespect and—at its strongest—hatred of the other. Under such a regime, dynamic balance can never be achieved. Similarly, monocultures replace biodiverse ecosystems in the same way as pornography replaces a multiverse which acknowledges the different experiences had by people who do not fit the youthful male, heterosexual, mobile and middle-class mainstream model. Just as 'whiteness' has been critiqued, so too 'masculinity' and the institutional supports of masculinity need to be considered.[15]

---

15 For critiques of racism and whiteness see Morrison (1993), Jensen (2005); for critiques of masculinity, see Stoltenberg (1990), Jensen (2005), Barry (2010).

8
Free trade and free speech

> Word by word, *elles* establishes itself as a sovereign subject. Only then could *il(s)*, *they-he*, appear reduced and truncated out of language.
>
> —Monique Wittig, 'The Mark of Gender' in *The Straight Mind and Other Essays* (1985, p. 85)

It is an interesting observation that the proponents of free trade are in many instances also the proponents of free speech. But the word 'free' is ambiguous and its context determines whether free has something to do with liberty, or more to do with a 'free-for-all'. In the case of 'free trade', exploitation of the poor, the colonised and the less powerful lies at the root of the word 'free'. Likewise, the term 'free speech' sounds innocuous, indeed is frequently made to sound politically important to a state of social freedom, but when one looks a little closer, 'whose' freedom counts, becomes the determining factor of whether it really represents the idea of 'freedom'.

Free trade agreements have ensured that the powerful economies have no roadblocks to trading wherever and whenever they wish. Small economies are left languishing and become dependent on corporations. As a long-term critic of free trade agreements I am concerned not only with the effects on trade but also the language used in the treaties.

The language of 'free trade' and 'free choice' misrepresents the idea of 'freedom' as one that is closely intertwined with responsibility. Within the realm of neo-classical economics, globalisation and free-trade mantras of transnational companies, freedom has no association with responsibility at all. In the world of international trade, transnational companies, the US government and institutions such as the World Trade Organization are playing a free and irresponsible game. As the more powerful players they get to make the rules, tip the playing field so that it is not level, and score the game as well (Hawthorne, 2003a, p. 29).

Nothing has changed for the better since I wrote these words, indeed, if anything, the Global Financial Crisis of 2008 has contributed to an even more tilted playing field. Hardly anyone bothers to keep score any more because then it would be far too obvious that the winner takes all. Indeed, 'disaster capitalism' appears to have become the favoured modus operandi (Klein, 2007).

Publishing has replicated this pattern of free trade with an ever-increasing size of megapublishing and megabookselling corporations. In Italy, Mondadori is the biggest publishing house in the country and is controlled by Fininvest, the family holding company of former Italian President, Silvio Berlusconi. His daughter, Marina Berlusconi, is the Chairman [*sic*]. The intersection of political power and publishing is not unusual, as Rupert Murdoch has so ably shown through his interference in the media in the UK, USA and Australia. Both these examples represent the worst excesses of so-called free trade and free speech. I say 'so-called' because in both cases there have been ample instances of interference in the trade and speech of others.

A major proponent of free speech has turned out to be the pornography and prostitution industry: the purveyors of women's so-called free sexuality. In fact, this defence, which is most often heard in the USA where free speech is constitutionally guaranteed, is really about guaranteeing their freedom to exploit, to sell and to brutalise prostituted people (the vast majority of whom are female). When feminists criticise pornographers, they are said to be limiting the freedom of speech of pornographers. The mouthpiece of the industry is the Free Speech Coalition, founded in 1991 to protect the adult entertainment and pornography industries from curtailment of their 'free speech'. In their media and press releases, they use the language of rights and civil liberties, a complete distortion of these ideas which were, and are, used by the powerless to fight the powerful. This has now been completely reversed. If legislators and philosophers would consider the logical and socially ethical reasoning of feminists, in this instance the very useful concept of 'fair speech' (McLellan, 2010), they would not find themselves defending abusers of 'free speech' because they are so scared of infringing the USA's First Amendment guaranteeing free speech.

"People do have a right to be bigots," proclaimed Australia's Attorney-General George Brandis in the Senate on 23 March 2014 (Harrison and Swan, 2014). He was arguing in favour of the Liberal government's proposed repeal of Section 18C of the Racial Discrimination Act.[16] The Act protects those who are

---

16 In 2011, right-wing journalist Andrew Bolt was prosecuted for breaching the racial vilification laws under Section 18C of the Racial Discrimination Act. His lawyers, and subsequently George Brandis, have argued that media commentators should have greater freedom of expression. This view has been challenged by Indigenous, Jewish, Muslim and immigrant

subjected to offence, insult, humiliation or intimidation on the grounds of race (ComLaw, 2013).

While the subject of speech acts has had significant airing in Australia, sadly the parameters of the discussion are so flawed that the most that can be said is that if Section 18C of the Racial Discrimination Act were repealed or amended, there would be more public abuse by the powerful of those already subjected to hate speech. Instead of problematising 'free speech', Brandis and others claim their right to bigotry. The freedom to be a bigot takes precedence over fairness in social relations. If the concept of 'fair speech' were introduced into the argument, the shape of the discussion would change. Fairness and justice should take precedence.

communities around the country. It has also been critiqued by feminist, disability, LGBTI and human rights organisations.

9
Fair trade and fair speech

> [H]ow few are willing to give up the power
> relationship. Even the powerless cling to the
> ideology, in the hope that as long as the *idea* exists
> they have hope of escaping power*less*ness by
> achieving *some*way, *some*how, power*ful*ness.
> Of course, as long as the conceptual framework
> of 'power' itself is valued (especially, if valued by
> the Oppressed!) none of us has any hope.
>
> —Ti-Grace Atkinson, *Amazon Odyssey* (1974, p. xxii)

There are two ways of approaching equality: action based on 'equality of opportunity', and action based on 'equality of outcomes'.

In liberal jurisdictions, a great deal of effort is put into creating equality of *opportunity*. What this means is that jobs are open to all who have the required qualifications (inherently associated with the system of meritocracy). Equality of opportunity frequently fails the oppressed because while they may all walk in the same door, those in the dominant group are more likely to make it to the other side of the room faster. In the case of men and women, men are more likely to get the jobs, and more likely to be promoted more quickly than any woman in a comparable position (assuming she was able to get roughly the same education and qualifications to start with).

Equality of opportunity looks as though it is doing something about inequality but, in fact, all the structures of discrimination maintain the overall inequities between people. For this to change, equality of *outcomes* must be used. But, say the apologists for inequality, that would be unfair. It is odd that those who make these arguments can often be found among race-goers who readily accept the idea of 'handicaps' when it is applied to horse racing. Why? Because if you could be sure which horse would win, no one would bother going to the races, and where would the gambling industry be then?

Equality of outcomes ensures uncertainty about who will get the job. It is also used in the Paralympics in order to equalise the chances of athletes with different abilities. If used in the work-force, people from non-dominant ethnic groups, women, the poor and the disabled, as well as the old and the young, would have improved chances of getting jobs.

In the literature industry, some countries offer grants to publishers to support the publication of writers. This is the case in Australia where the Australia Council for the Arts gives grants to publishing houses who publish literary works by Australian writers. Multinational publishers have equal opportunity in applying for and receiving such grants, even though their turnover may be hundreds of times greater than that of the small and independent publisher. No account is taken of this differential. The rules of the World Trade Organisation (WTO) mean that companies should not be discriminated against when governments provide such subsidies unless the government has specified it in their variations on rules.[17]

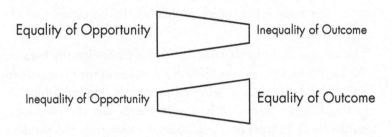

How is this relevant to publishing? Its relevance comes into the debate on free expression. What is called 'free speech' is often nothing more than the ability of the powerful to speak their views very loudly and forcefully, and thereby drown out the views, the opinions and the free speech of those they do not wish to hear.

In *Unspeakable* (2010), Betty McLellan draws parallels between free trade / fair trade and free speech / fair speech. Here, in brief, are her main points:

- free trade / free speech favours the powerful
- free trade / free speech fosters and entrenches inequality
- free trade / free speech focuses on the individual
- free trade / free speech ignores quality of life (pp. 52–58).

McLellan does not specifically articulate the contrasting axioms, but the consequences of her ideas are as follows:

- fair trade / fair speech decentralises power

---

17 For further reading on the WTO, see Hawthorne (2002); on General Agreement on Trade in Services (GATS), see Hawthorne (2005); on cultural trade, see Australia Council (2002).

- fair trade / fair speech fosters justice and fair treatment
- fair trade / fair speech focuses on the common good and engagement
- fair trade / fair speech highlights the importance of life over profit.

Her arguments fit nicely with the idea of bibliodiversity because fair speech fosters the possibility of the voices of the marginalised being heard or read. As indicated previously, 'big publishing' in general repeats formulaic best sellers with just the occasional outlier voice. Independent publishers, who are truly independent and not in receipt of support from corporate, educational, religious or other forms of sponsorship tied to what they can say, publish the risky, the innovative, the controversial, the marginal and the imaginative voices.

Fair speech is precisely what the International Alliance of Independent Publishers means when they say:

> We openly declare our solidarity with all of our publishing colleagues, with authors, and with all other book professionals who today still suffer intimidation, psychological or physical violence, or threat of imprisonment—all of which endangers their work, if not their lives. We note as well the development of less direct forms of censorship, whether they result from bureaucracy (customs blockages, arbitrary taxation), legal or financial causes, or as they arise from a mechanism of self-censorship. The phenomenon of concentration and of commercialization in the book publishing sector, in media, and in communications also contributes directly or indirectly to reinforcing or reviving forms of censorship (2007, p. 7).

Just as equality of opportunity maintains the status quo, free trade in a globalised economy is massively advantageous to those who already have global resources. Their ability to trade freely is supported by international agreements developed by the large economies for their own advantage.

Free speech, when resorted to by Rupert Murdoch or a pornographer, silences those who do not have media empires behind them. The voices of prostituted women are drowned out; the so-called unions purportedly working on behalf of prostitutes turn out to have a majority membership of pimps and brothel owners (Ekis Ekman, 2013, pp. 59–78). What other industry has employers running the union? Certainly this occurs, but when it is called out, it is rarely defended.

An analysis of fair speech must also consider the effects of silencing. Censorship is not only the straightforward culling and banning of the words of writers and artists, and the imprisonment, torture or killing of those who utter rebellious words. It also ventures into the realm of social conditioning. In *Pornography and Silence* (1982), Susan Griffin makes the connection between the violence of pornography and women's silence. She argues that the silence is as much internal as external. This is also the case for colonised peoples in general. Judy Atkinson (2002) outlines the generational trauma inflicted on Indigenous people, which is passed on generation by generation. Those from the working class are familiar with similar kinds of transgenerational trauma, as are people marginalised by hatred (in a Christian-dominant world, Jews and Muslims have suffered this fate).

For a publishing industry to foster bibliodiversity all this must be taken into account. The upshot is that women's voices must be heard, as must the voices of people who have been historically marginalised: the colonised, peasants and workers. As Maria Mies and colleagues so presciently noted in 1988:

> The realization that the women's question is related to the colonial question and that both are related to the dominant, global, capitalist-patriarchal model of accumulation, did not dawn upon us suddenly or in our studies. Our perception of the systematic relationship between these questions is the result of many years of experience in the Third World (in India and Latin America) and involvement in women's struggles in Europe (Mies, Bennholdt-Thomsen and von Werlhof, pp. 1–2).

The global publishing industry thrives on the subaltern marginal voice[18] because those existing on the margins—like the wild seeds—have a new ideational energy for the society. But it is often short-lived, a fashion, something exotic (Hawthorne, 1989) or shocking. More challenging is the possibility of those same marginal people taking over the means of production. As the publisher of a feminist press, that is exactly our intent. While, in large publishing houses, women play significant roles in editorial and promotion, being in charge of creating a dynamic balance in areas such as production, management, distribution, warehousing, technology and sales is far more daunting and less likely to occur.

Publishers used to depend on book reviews, especially in-depth reviews in daily metropolitan newspapers followed up by essays in literary and current affairs magazines. When I was a regular reviewer in the mid- to late 1980s, a standard review for

---

18 The winners of the Booker and Mann Booker Prize give a clue to this. While there are British winners of the prize, the number of winners from former British colonies creates new markets for these outlier voices.

a single book was 800–1,000 words in length. Review space has been dramatically reduced and while online blogs or social media sites have taken up some of the slack, overall the importance of reviews has declined, and instead of a broad readership, social media appeals to niche markets. Prizes, in the meantime, have proliferated, but only a few of these have the potential to increase sales. Independent publishers have often used niche media to good effect in the past, but now multinationals looking for new markets are trespassing on these media. Similarly, festivals are now being held everywhere, with mixed results.

An analogous example to 'fair speech' that applies specifically to the publishing industry is the Forest Council's system of approval for the use of FSC and PEFC logos in the printing of books.[19] In order for a book to have an FSC or PEFC logo it must be *approved* before it is printed. This is because the 'fair forestry' system recognises the importance of preventing the profligate use of resources on massively wasteful print advertising—junk mail, catalogues for over-consumptive goods, and other print material that the Forest Council deems unacceptable. It probably won't be long before cries of discrimination are heard from anti-ecologists, though I wonder what arguments they would use to justify their over-use of scarce sustainable forests for over-consumption of unnecessary and uneconomical materials.

The International Alliance of Independent Publishers calls for publishers to consider the environment in the Declaration of Paris:

---

19 FSC (Forest Stewardship Council) and PEFC (Programme for the Endorsement of Forest Certification) are both environmental programs intended to reduce waste as well as unsustainable forestry. The former is a strong system, and the latter is the certification system used by many small forest owners.

"We are aware that, even while we struggle for and insist on our rights, we must also affirm our own duties and responsibilities—whether they be cultural, social or environmental" (International Alliance of Independent Publishers, 2007, p. 7). Publishers in rich countries must, however, recognise that those working in poorer nations might not always be able to access ecologically sustainable paper.

'Fair speech', 'fair trade', 'sustainable forestry', and 'fair book'[20] are all terms that put justice and fairness at the centre of decision-making.

The implications of an 'ethic of speech' (McLellan, 2010), or more precisely, an ethic of *fair* speech, are serious ones for publishers. And if fair speech and fair trade could be made central to the business of publishing, not only would we have a fairer system in place, but authors would get a fairer hearing; authors who have new or different things to say would have a voice; independent publishers would get fairer deals instead of being pushed to the margins; and perhaps readers would return to a flourishing independent world of bookshops where they could find non-homogenised books to read, books to expand their horizons.[21]

---

20 This term is used by the International Alliance of Independent Publishers for co-editions, and translations between members in which support is given to assist the project's fruition.

21 One reviewer who has taken this task seriously is M.D. Brady, whose 'Me, You and Books' blog bristles with books reviewed from around the world. See <http://mdbrady.wordpress.com/>. I attempted something similar with my regular column in the *Australian Women's Book Review* in the early 1990s.

10
Recolonisation

> Making the nation-state safe for multinational corporations is commensurate with making it safe for heterosexuality, for both can be recodified as natural, even supernatural. Thus tourism and imperialism become as integral to the natural order as heterosexuality, and are indispensable in state strategies of recolonization.
>
> —M. Jacqui Alexander, *Pedagogies of Crossing* (2005, p. 26)

The 'digital revolution' has not only opened the doors to small players, but created new opportunities for megapublishing and megabookselling to recolonise those who have worked hard to decolonise themselves and their communities over the last century. Decolonisation meant throwing off cultural cringe, validating and celebrating dispossessed peoples and cultures, including languages prohibited by the colonisers. Indigenous languages, for example, have battled to have their own words published by those who respect their meanings and their contexts. This is a battle that has been fought in Africa, in South America, in the Basque lands, among the colonised everywhere, and in the English-language colonies of Australia, Canada, USA, South Africa and Aotearoa/New Zealand. A recent example in the Australian media has been a critical examination of the words 'dreaming' and 'dreamtime' (Nicholls, 2014). Nicholls argues that at the core is a distortion of the original meaning expressed differently in at least 250 languages in pre-colonised Australia. Such misuse of words has implications for how Aboriginal societies are perceived and their ideas and concepts understood. Some languages are targeted as the languages of terrorists— the Basque language has suffered this fate. Elsewhere in the 'developing world', as the International Alliance of Independent Publishers puts it,

> books in African languages have a potentially wide market. However, some barriers considerably reduce the size of this potential readership, amongst others, high illiteracy rates, the absence of reading habits, the weak buying power of the targeted public and the low visibility / availability of publications (2013b).

The availability of books in local and national languages is an issue for colonised peoples from around the world. Colonialism is a heavy heritage and difficult to throw off because infrastructures are put in place to assist the already powerful. Media and education can be used for ill or for good. For example, when engaging in a distribution deal with the big digital players, the contractual expectations are those that are in the interest of the megacorporations. In the English-language market this is exemplified in contracts that put the USA at the centre and pay no heed to smaller markets outside the behemoth of US publishing.

In Africa, independent publishers have protested the dumping of books into their markets. In French-speaking Gabon, Cameroun, Mali, and Niger, for example, books in the official French language are dumped under the guise of providing reading material to desperately poor children and their schools; books written, produced and published in France are 'donated'. Smaller independent and locally-based publishers cannot afford to donate books to schools on a massive scale and, as a result, are locked out of what could otherwise be an important source of income, one that would ensure the survival of the home-grown publisher with local knowledge (International Alliance of Independent Publishers, 2013a). Furthermore, the developing world has facile mainstream books dumped on them, in a way that is similar to the dumping of products rejected by the West, such as cigarettes and ineffective and dangerous pharmaceuticals. In Brazil, the apparently charitable donation of books by banks is actually little more than a marketing tool, and the books are very low quality. It results in the 'donation' of junk and torn books. Instead of banks buying good books to donate to libraries they spend millions on the advertising campaign. Furthermore, the challenges of distribution are such that, frequently, publishers are not paid. Instead the massively supported educational publishers take the largest slice of the cake (Araken Gomes Ribeiro, 2013, pers. comm.).

These actions are anathema to the spirit of bibliodiversity. By contrast, as the International Alliance of Independent Publishers has stated, "independent publishers guarantee the multiplicity and circulation of ideas, and as such are the real players and defenders of this cultural diversity within publishing" (2007, p. 4).

Bibliodiversity is not just about numbers. It is also about patterning and process. It is not just about producing books differently, it is about an entirely different social context for ideas. The free expression of ideas needs to be balanced against the common good (Roy, 1999; Mies and Bennholdt-Thomsen, 1999; Shiva, 2012). The concept of fair speech (McLellan, 2010) can assist us in finding that balancing point.

Like ecology, publishing is part of a complex system that responds to the changing forces in the world. Independent publishers often have a knack for anticipating cultural shifts. This is because they ride the fast-moving outer shoreline of the cultural river while the big publishers paddle in the shallow mainstream.

Publishing is at a crossroads. We now have access to relatively cheap production processes that let giant publishers, such as Penguin Random House, Hachette, Mondadori and others, flood the market with their books. But the same production processes also allow marginal voices to speak. This is borne out by the huge increase in short-run and digital poetry publishing. And self-publishing, in the tradition of the modernists, is now more available than ever. In concert with these changes in production, the digital distribution of a single voice can have a global reach. As Suniti Namjoshi noted in 1996, a writer can now say: "I am broadcasting to the world. Not just my vote, but my voice, my VOICE is being heard". But there is a problem. "Is anyone listening to my broadcast?" (pp. xxiv–xxv).

An individual with access to a computer can build a global audience through blogs, websites and social networking. And while such individual reach is rare, a single voice can spread like a virus through a global audience.

But self-publishing too has been appropriated, and much of it is now in the hands of Amazon. Traditional publishing involves a contract agreed upon by publisher and author, and although there have been many disgruntled authors who have signed up to contracts they later regretted, at least the publisher is obliged to obtain the consent of the author to change those conditions. Amazon, by contrast, reserves the right to change any part of its contract, for any reason, at any time with any author who has signed on. Writers need to inform themselves about the pitfalls of these new kinds of contracts.

Against recolonisation we should bear in mind the words of Arundhati Roy:

> Our strategy should be not only to confront empire, but to lay siege to it. To deprive it of oxygen. To shame it. To mock it. With our art, our music, our literature, our stubbornness, our joy, our brilliance, our sheer relentlessness—and our ability to tell our own stories. Stories that are different from the ones we're being brainwashed to believe (2003, p. 112).

We could all be drowned out in the static of digital publishing if we don't create networks now to assist in the spread of the voices of bibliodiversity. Can we answer the question raised by Suniti Namjoshi in 1996: "Is anyone listening to my broadcast?" Do the blogs, eBooks, apps for iPads, tablets, tweets, phone fiction, websites and a host of other possibilities that are streaming into our homes and workplaces aid us in having our voices heard? Small publishers have the advantage of flexibility and smaller lists to convert or create. Through our websites we can make literature available directly to our readers and we can engage with those readers.[22] It is my hope that bibliodiversity will extend into this new digital space.

---

22 Problems remain with digital distribution. See p. 60 below.

We need to do battle with those purveyors of monopsony, a position held by Amazon, whose practices are distorting the marketplace (Kohn, 2014). There are major skirmishes occurring between the large publishers and the large retailers. When Apple entered the market in 2010 it looked as if Amazon's monopsony might be challenged, but as Bob Kohn points out:

> All was well until the Justice Department, supported by a white paper supplied to it by Amazon, filed an ill-advised lawsuit against Apple and five of the major book publishers for antitrust violations. The publishers were charged with 'price fixing'—but not for fixing prices: Not a single e-book price was fixed by the conspiracy contrived by the government. All the publishers did, as I argued in a friend-of-the-court brief at the time, was to move to the lawful app store model, which eliminated Amazon's self-serving distortion of the e-book market (2014).

The contradictory positions of megapublishers and independent publishers requires the latter to walk the tightrope between flexibility and early adoption of new technologies, and the 'need' for wide distribution, which is almost totally in the hands of some of the most powerful and capitalised companies in the world.

In the world of contemporary globalised publishing we are facing the massive market power of one player: Amazon. Not only does Amazon have distorting power as a *buyer*—of books and eBooks from publishers (monopsony); but also as the most powerful *seller*—of books and other consumer goods to consumers (monopoly). This market power does not represent the competitive model so favoured by neoclassical economists; rather, it is much more like the power of the sugar industry in South America that Eduard Galeano (1973) refers to in his exposé of 500 years of Latin American history, or of the East India Company under British colonial rule, or the power of Monsanto in the agribusiness industry. It is indeed a matter of recolonising our markets and our minds.

11
Digital bibliodiversity

> [Co-publishing] has to do with economic viability.
> We are talking of co-publishing not just as
> making it possible for a book or an author to be
> published simultaneously across the world, in
> one language or many languages, we are also
> talking of economics; the economics of doing
> something like this, and co-publishing as one way
> of arriving at something viable.
>
> —Ritu Menon, 'Coedición Simultánea de Libros
> Feministas' (1990, p. 102)

The digital system—as opposed to the industrial system—reflects organic patterns and processes in the way in which it operates. But just as 'big pharma' has been able to colonise and appropriate the knowledge of indigenous and traditional peoples in order to make massive profits, so too the digital system can be appropriated, distorted, corporatised and privatised by 'big publishing'. Indeed, this is precisely what is being done right now.

Digital is first and foremost a system of networks—the Internet and social networking systems exemplify this. While I am not a 'tech head', I have seen how ready access to mobile phones has affected the lives of many people in India and Bangladesh. People living in poverty use technology in different ways. In remote Indigenous communities in Australia, communal access to computers enables communication across deserts. In rural Indonesia, an elderly woman is able to contact a relative in another village by asking her son to send an email. A young woman in India or Nigeria can access digital books on her mobile phone.

Between the megapublishers, micropublishers are also proliferating. They are like the small green plants that come up between the cracks in the concrete. Some of these will grow and become the publishers for a particular social group or geographical location. Through networking it is possible for this material to reach wider audiences. With a new generation of digital natives, digital publishing will become the norm. At present, few publishers would report more than 20 per cent of their sales as digital, while 80 per cent remain as print sales. The time frame in which this change will take place is hard to predict, but I suspect those figures will reverse in some markets in the next couple of decades. There are already publishers who only produce digital titles. But print books will continue, I have no doubt about that: books as gifts, as stores of knowledge to ponder, as novels to take to the beach, as picture books to put into the hands of children, and as poetry; as small luxury items to cherish.

What remains important, whatever the means of production or reading, is the content—that is the crux of bibliodiversity and the core business of independent publishers.

If 'big distribution'—and there is increasing concentration in the hands of fewer and fewer companies, including across language boundaries—is reduced to a handful of players, then the advantages of networking for small players will vanish.[23] Some will be able to survive because of temporary loyalty, but loyalty tends to be generational and that too will shift over time.

It is therefore critical that independent writers, publishers, artists, designers, media, booksellers, librarians and independent-minded readers realise the importance of cross-sector support.[24]

There is a confusion going on in the publishing industry. Major book retailers want to be publishers; major publishers want to be book retailers. Convergence does not benefit authors nor independent publishers and booksellers. But it is 'sold' to those at the distributive bottom of the pile as a great advantage: the advantage of reaching a global market; the advantage of no print costs. But most of these 'advantages' are elusive. How will the small player reach the global audience? How will they avoid the costs of design, editing, proofreading, typesetting, marketing and distribution? Will readers want to read badly edited books? Will they want to read books in which design issues are not considered? Will marketing and online distribution be enough? The so-called advantage is then used as a way of extracting the most successful of those self-published writers, or the most successful of the independents, by buying them up. In 2011, Penguin acquired Bookworld from REDGroup Retail (formerly a part of Borders

---

23 On 14 March 2014, Amazon announced that it will produce German-language books; Penguin Random House now publishes in English, German and Spanish.

24 To this end the International Alliance of Independent Publishers has run workshops for publishers, including one that specifically addressed the needs of Arabic-language publishers (International Alliance Independent Publishers, 2014b). It also undertook an international study in 2010–2011 on 'Digital Publishing in the Developing World' (Kulesz, 2011).

and Angus & Robertson). Bookworld is the fastest growing online bookstore in Australia and now a subsidiary of Penguin Random House Australia. Similar arrangements exist between other major publishing houses in many different language markets. At the other end of the spectrum, superstores such as Amazon are setting up online publishing arms. It began in 2009 with AmazonEncore and there are now thirteen imprints.

A further phenomenon is the online self-publisher with a global product. *Fifty Shades of Grey* by E.L. James is one such example, and the three-book series is published by Random House which, since its merger with Penguin Books, is now the biggest English-language publisher in the world. It is also the owner of Goldmann, the German publisher of *Fifty Shades of Grey*. When *Publishers Weekly* named E.L. James as 'Publishing Person of the Year' in 2012 there was an outcry of despair from some quarters of the publishing industry concerned about what counts as 'literature'. From the critical point of view of bibliodiversity this despair is well-founded. E.L. James simply hit upon a winning formula at the right time: a retelling of an age-old misogynist fairy tale of a dominating, sadistic man and a beautiful, poor, masochistic woman (Hawthorne, 2012b).

Another example of a small company being taken over by a big one is the (formerly) Australian company Booki.sh. Booki.sh created a digital cloud-based reading platform, and it experimented with digital selling of independent publishers' books through independent booksellers. It was a great success. It is now owned by OverDrive, a US-based company that supplies books to the international library market. Access to the Booki.sh platform for independent publishers and booksellers was assigned to OverDrive. The sale was a smart business decision for the company owners, but the consequences for independent publishing and bookselling in Australia have been significant. Independent booksellers lost a platform for selling eBooks, and independent publishers lost a locally run outlet for selling their eBooks.[25]

The language used in this acquisition is interesting. Steve Potash, CEO and President of OverDrive, said:

> The Booki.sh team have created a fresh, direct and immersive reading experience that uniquely serves the mission of our libraries and schools. Its innovative technologies streamline the access and convenience of e-books, which will help shape how millions of readers and students enjoy e-books from OverDrive's network of thousands of libraries, schools and booksellers in over 20 countries (cited in Kozlowski, 2014).

Independence helped Booki.sh achieve great success, and I commend them for their creativity and intelligence. Words like 'fresh', 'direct', and 'innovative' are rarely applied to megapublishing. As Timothy Swanson (1996) says of biodiversity, the corporations rely on the 'wild' in biodiversity and, in a similar way, the big publishers rely on the 'fresh' in bibliodiversity, for their new advances. Originality comes from the margins, from the independent; the small sustains the big. It remains to be seen whether OverDrive will be able to live up to the ambitions and hopes of Booki.sh.

---

25 The members of the Small Press Network, in conjunction with a group of independent bookstores, worked successfully with Booki.sh from 2011–2012 (Booki.sh, 2014).

12
Organic publishing

> [T]he goal of Nayakrishi Andolon [New Agricultural
> Movement] is not to produce more food for
> consumers, but to create life, diversity and *ananda*
> [to live a happy life].
>
> —Farida Akhter, 'Resisting "Technology" and Defending
> Subsistence in Bangladesh' (2001, p. 392)

The ecology of publishing is an issue that will stretch the minds of independent publishers in the coming decades. While megapublishing will entail more and more mergers, increased digitisation, convergence of book retailers and book publishers, and massive multilingual homogenised publishing, at the other end will be the small-scale publishers: independents and self-publishers.

Writing and publishing are frequently at their best as small-scale ventures, just as organic farming has its best results when done on limited acreage. Staying small enables the farmer to produce something unique, a flavour or colour that can't be re-produced industrially. In the mainstream, one hears big business arguing that 'organic' is 'only for the rich', and by farming on an industrial scale agribusiness can produce food that the poor can afford. Farida Akhter in Bangladesh, however, has shown by example how people with few resources also ought to be able to eat healthy food, food grown without pesticides and without the intervention of companies like Monsanto (Akhter, 2001; Robin, 2010).

Thinking about the connections between the environment and publishing, one is struck by several similarities. A significant example is that of paper. Most of the world's paper is produced from plantation forests, the majority of which are made up of exotic species, clear-felled to maximise profits for the forestry companies. The first destruction is that of native forests replaced by plantations of exotic trees. Second-level destruction occurs when the plantation trees are clear-felled. Clear-felling wreaks destruction in a similar way to bombing. It is the destruction of forest ecosystems because not only are the large trees felled, but undergrowth, micro-organisms, and soils are destroyed too. The bigger the publishing company, the bigger the print runs, and subsequently the more paper used. New print technology could help here by making it more viable to have short-run books, that is, books with print runs of 100–700 copies. Short runs reduce the unnecessary use of paper resources. Many of the large print runs also incur large pulping numbers: wasted books, wasted paper, wasted trees.

In the publishing industry it is possible for booksellers to return unsold stock to the publisher. This is an incredibly wasteful practice and is sometimes due to over-subscription of books, especially by superstores and chains. Not only does it lead to a waste of paper, but also the unnecessary use of oil and diesel in transporting books back and forth along already congested roads (or by other means) when the books are returned, deemed in excess, and then pulped.

Small independents are less likely to engage in excessive print runs, and while they might not have any control over returns, because inflated subscriptions are far less likely, their contribution to waste is significantly less.

Continuing its taste for mergers, in March 2014 Random House announced it had purchased Spanish-language publisher Santillana. While there might be space for a few enterprising individuals in this super-large, tri-language publishing house, chances are that books will all begin to look the same (one author in three languages). The uniform tomatoes in the supermarket are like the look-alike books coming out of huge publishing houses. They have lost all local flavour, the language is mostly 'Americanised', and the characters float in a no-place globalised world suffering only the problems of the well-off. Or, they reproduce the various kinds of violence that those of us who have fought against racism, misogyny, colonisation and the like have refused to make profits from. The new cover of the 2013 reprint of Sylvia Plath's *The Bell Jar* (by Faber) is one such example: a globalised cover that turns the main character into a flimsy, all-American girl-next-door, when, in fact, *The Bell Jar* is about a young woman battling depression and anxiety because of the social expectations put upon her in a time that was unfriendly to feminism. This is part of the distortion of ideas that capitalism engages in. And while the text itself remains intact, the marketing of it distorts the author's intentions for the book. Given the author is not around to protest the distortion of her 'moral right', such unethical marketing appropriations will continue.

Organic publishing takes time. It means treating every book, and every writer of a book, in context. It means taking account of the author's intentions, not just throwing a cover on a book because it's the latest design fashion. Female writers are expected to accept sexualised 'chick lit' covers even when that is not how they would categorise their own work. Cover designers for the mainstream will produce 'boy' covers for men's books, and 'girl' covers for women's books (Flood, 2013). While some might argue that it's a suitable way to find appropriate markets for books, it can readily result in exoticising of 'foreign' books and condescending and patronising marketing of women's books.

I believe that organic publishing produces better books. If readers understood a little more about the politics and economics of publishing, perhaps more would take the risk of reading a book by an author who is unknown or from an unfamiliar place. Change requires both intention and follow through. As a reader, venturing only to the front of the bookshop is a bit like visiting Europe or Asia or Africa for five days. Exploring ideas takes time. You don't need to leave home, but you do need to seek out new concepts and perceptions of the world, as well as people you don't already know. Or, you need to dig deeper among those you do. To live on the surface can be all very glamorous but at some point it becomes tiring; satisfaction is lacking, one becomes cynical and despairing.

A publishing industry that is sustainable is one in which books have more than a three-month shelf life. The demands of ever more profits, highly mobile books, massive distribution warehouses, externalities of star author advances that need to be supported by star author international travel and national festival tours, do not contribute to an ecologically sustainable industry. Small is beautiful and so is independent.

13
Principles of bibliodiversity:
Patterns and processes[26]

> Self-organizing, nonlinear, feedback systems are
> inherently unpredictable. They are not controllable.
> They are understandable only in the most general
> way. The goal of foreseeing the future exactly and
> preparing for it perfectly is unrealizable ... The future
> can't be predicted, but it can be envisioned and
> brought lovingly into being.
>
> —Donella H. Meadows, *Thinking in Systems*
> (2008, pp. 167–169)

Networks

All cultural artefacts in an eco-social system are interconnected
through networks of relationship. In order for cultures to thrive,
networks must exist. For example, a poem can give rise to other
works of art, such as a musical composition, a painting, a dance
or an opera. Art works cross-pollinate. Traditional knowledges
pollinate contemporary artworks while contemporary work
feeds back into cultural knowledge. Independent and fresh ideas

---

26 This list has been adapted from Stone, Michael K. (n.d.) 'Ecological
Principles'.
See Meadows (2008) for another list of Systems Principles, especially
pp. 188–191.

pollinate the corporations. This could be useful if it were treated respectfully.

Nested systems

Culture is comprised of systems nested within other systems. While each system is complete in itself, it is also part of a larger system. Changes in one part of the system can affect other nested systems, as well as having an effect on the larger system. Publishing houses are nested within the larger system of writing, storytelling and literature which, in turn, is nested inside the specific culture, and again inside the global system of storytelling (which includes poetry, film, journalism, live performance, etc.). Publishing also exists within the nested system of corporate profit which is currently exerting more influence than that of culture; that is, the merchant has become more important than the culture, and the 'business of books', as André Schiffrin calls it, has turned more towards 'business' than to the content of books (Schiffrin, 2001; Thompson, 2010).

Cycles

Members of an eco-social system—a culture—depend on the continuous exchange of energy through ideas and storytelling. Cycles intersect within and between local, regional and global systems. A story about relationship exists on local and global levels.

Flows

Every culture—however small or large—needs a continual flow of ideational energy to thrive. The flow of energy from the natural world to the human world creates and sustains initial ideational and psychological forces resulting in language; for example, adults (mostly mothers) sing to their children, tell stories and indulge in nonsense talk. In this way, children learn to speak and tell their own stories.

Development

All culture—from a child's story to the global cultural industries—changes with the passage of time (or place). Stories build by accretion, variation, new interpretation, as well as new media for representation, for example: orature to literature (papyrus, palm leaf, hand-copied manuscripts); the printed book to the digital book.

Dynamic balance

Eco-social communities become dynamic feedback loops, so that while there is continuous fluctuation, a bibliodiverse and multiverse community maintains a reasonably steady state. Dynamic balance is the basis of cultural resilience. For example, when large publishers cease to publish poetry, a host of small DIY and independent outlets open up until the large publishers are prompted to think that this must be profitable and so, for a while, once again publish poetry.

14
Bibliodiversity in the twenty-first century

> Biodiversity cannot be conserved until diversity is
> made the logic of production.
>
> —Vandana Shiva, *Monocultures of the Mind*
> (1993, p. 146)

♦ "If I can't dance, I don't want to be part of your revolution"
  said Emma Goldman in 1931 (p. 207). I would add: "If poetry
  is no longer published, I don't want to be part of that kind of
  industry."
♦ The wild type is crucial to the existence and maintenance
  of biodiversity. Let us not exclude those who challenge our
  comfort zones.
♦ Dominant languages have a way of taking over. Not only
  by swamping local languages, but also by sidelining certain
  variations of the dominant language. Let us all learn at least
  one other language.
♦ Let us make a commitment to fair speech—not just free and
  loud speech.
♦ Let us commit to ensuring that both halves of humanity are
  part of our bibliodiverse societies. It will mean that men will
  have to learn to read and listen differently and even to think
  differently.
♦ Let us not just count numbers—for how do you count the
  number of copies sold for writers like Virginia Woolf and

Zora Neale Hurston in 1937; or for titles translated into English like Stieg Larsson and Mahmoud Darwish in 2000? Who will we count? Who will be the visible ones at the time of counting? Would we wish later that we had counted the difficult to find? The process of counting is tantamount to saying that only the countable are worth anything. This contradicts bibliodiversity.

♦ Let us recognise bibliodiverse hot spots rather than top-down marketing binges called 'festivals'.

♦ Let us ensure that we maintain and sustain bibliodiversity when we enter the digital publishing arena.

♦ Let us not recolonise.

♦ Let us ensure that we build rich soils so that the cultural forms, the stories, the content that retains its social integrity, are maintained and sustained.

♦ Let us challenge international trade rules that give preference to corporate infrastructures.

♦ Let us commit to equality of outcome.

♦ Let us support independence of approach across the sector: authors, translators, publishers, distributors, reviewers, booksellers, librarians and the media.

Bibliodiversity, if it is truly to be based on the idea of biodiversity as first envisioned by Chilean publishers, must turn ecological principles into socio-ecological principles.[27] These principles,

---

27 André Schiffrin commented in an interview: "There's an attempt to get the green idea of biodiversity to extend to ideas—they call it 'bibliodiversity'. For instance, in Chile, around forty independent publishers got together under that label about ten years ago, and they have managed to preserve the necessary diversity of the editorial output available to readers over there" (Pouliquen and Testard, 2010).

as outlined above, are about complex living systems that are constantly in flux, reflecting the ever-changing shape of natural and cultural shifts. Our abuses of nature are resulting in an over-heated planet driving headlong towards severe climate change. Our abuses of culture are resulting in increasing levels of violence, reflected in books that are the cultural equivalent of climate change: promoting hatred and misogyny, monocultural violence against the 'other', and war-mongering.

I have no doubt that independent publishing will continue even in the face of global corporatisation and megapublishing. Like the fungi that grow in a circle around the roots of old trees—rising, falling, regenerating, creating necessary micro-organisms which sustain the soil—small and independent publishers will go on publishing risky, innovative and long-lasting books out of passion for literature. Books from now for the future.

Acknowledgements

My thanks go to the International Alliance of Independent Publishers, based in Paris with its networks of independent publishers in many continents. Particular thanks to Laurence Hugues and Juan Carlos Sáez for their insightful and thoughtful comments on the text. Also to all the individual members of publishing houses whose ideas were expressed at meetings and who gave me the energy to write this manifesto. While they have contributed to my thinking, they are not responsible for the final shape of this book.

I express my thanks to all the independent publishers I've worked with over many years. They come from numerous countries: Bangladesh, Chile, India, Germany, South Africa, USA, Aotearoa/New Zealand, Canada, Turkey, UK—and more. Special thanks to all the feminist publishers and booksellers, past and present, who helped me learn my trade in the early years. Their achievements still inspire me. Renate Klein and I have taken this journey together since founding Spinifex Press in 1991. I could not have travelled as far without her enthusiasm, passion and love. Thanks also to all the women who have made Spinifex what it is. To Renate, Pauline Hopkins and Maree Hawken, thank you for your fine editorial skills.

I have been thinking about the issues in this manifesto for several decades and much of what I know about international trade rules was learnt while undertaking my PhD. The real understanding comes from working in the trade, reflecting on our collective experience as feminist and independent publishers. As I finish this manifesto, it occurs to me that this is only a start. Each chapter of this small book could be expanded. We need more research about independent booksellers, translators, librarians, media commentators, and all who create the ideas and images, without whom we would not have a publishing industry.

I have previously expressed some of these ideas in different contexts and publications, including the following:

2002. *Wild Politics: Feminism, Globalisation and Bio/diversity*. Melbourne: Spinifex Press.

2011. 'Indicators of Bibliodiversity: A multiversalist's matrix'. *Bibliodiversity* 1. January. pp. 86–95. <http://www. bibliodiversity.org/Bibliodiversity%20Indicators.pdf>.

2011. 'Publishing Change see Digital see Bibliodiversity'. Invited Keynote Speaker. Australia New Zealand Society of Indexers Annual Conference, Melbourne. 12 September.

2012. 'Bibliodiversity: The power of the local in the global'. SPUNC Conference. Wheeler Centre, Melbourne. 8 November.

2013. 'Independent publishers around the world: Scenario, perspectives, bibliodiversity'. International Alliance of Independent Publishers Roundtable with publishers from Brazil, South Africa and Switzerland. Frankfurt Book Fair. 9 October.

2014. 'Fair Trade and Fair Speech: Feminist publishing in the 21st century'. Wheeler Centre for Books, Writing, Ideas. Melbourne. 19 March.

Bibliography

Akhter, Farida. 2001. 'Resisting "Technology" and Defending Subsistence in Bangladesh: Nayakrishi Andolon and the movement for a happy life'. In Bennholdt-Thomsen, Nicholas Faraclas and Claudia von Werlhof (eds). *There Is an Alternative: Subsistence and Worldwide Resistance to Corporate Globalization*. London: Zed Books; Melbourne: Spinifex Press. Also see UBINIG website: <http://www.ubinig.org/>.

Alexander, M. Jacqui. 2005. *Pedagogies of Crossing: Meditations on Feminism, Sexual Politics, Memory and the Sacred*. Durham and London: Duke University Press.

Anzaldúa, Gloria. 1987. *Borderlands/La Frontera: The New Mestiza*. San Francisco: Spinsters/Aunt Lute.

Asante, Molefe Kete. 1999. *The Painful Demise of Eurocentrism: An Afrocentric Response*. Trenton, NJ and Asmara, Ethiopia: Africa World Press.

Atkinson, Judy. 2002. *Trauma Trails, Recreating Song Lines: The Transgenerational Effects of Trauma in Indigenous Australia*. Melbourne: Spinifex Press.

Atkinson, Ti-Grace. 1974. *Amazon Odyssey*. New York: Links Books.

Australia Council. 2002. *Cultural Trade Background Report*. Sydney: Australia Council.

Barry, Kathleen. 2010. *Unmaking War Remaking Men*. Santa Rosa, CA: Phoenix Rising Press; Melbourne: Spinifex Press.

Bell, Diane. 1983/2002. *Daughters of the Dreaming*. Melbourne: Spinifex Press.

Bell, Diane. 1998/2014. *Ngarrindjeri Wurruwarrin: A World That Is, Was, and Will Be*. Melbourne: Spinifex Press.

Bell, Diane and Renate Klein (eds). 1996. *Radically Speaking: Feminism Reclaimed*. Melbourne: Spinifex Press.

Bell, Genevieve. 2001. 'A Theory of Shopping: A feminist reading of eCommerce'. Paper presented at George Washington University, Washington DC. 7 June.

Benhamou, Françoise. 2009. 'Les Assises et leurs suites. Comptes rendus des Assises internationales de l'édition indépendante et programme prévisionnel d'action 2008–2009 de l'Alliance des éditeurs indépendants'. International Alliance of Independent Publishers. 7 October. pp. 28–29.

Booki.sh. 2014. More about Booki.sh. <http://about.booki.sh/support/press>.

Bray, Abigail. 2013. *Misogyny Re-Loaded*. Melbourne: Spinifex Press.

Brodribb, Somer. 1992. *Nothing Mat(t)ers: A Feminist Critique of Postmodernism*. Melbourne: Spinifex Press.

Cacho, Lydia. 2012. *Slavery Inc.: The Untold Story of International Sex Trafficking*. Translated by Elizabeth Boburg. London: Portobello Books.

Carson, Rachel. 1962. *Silent Spring*. Harmondsworth, UK: Penguin Books.

Catton, Eleanor. 2013a. *The Luminaries*. London: Granta.

Catton, Eleanor. 2013b. 'Eleanor Catton on literature and elitism'. *Metro*. March. <http://metromag.co.nz/metro-archive/eleanor-catton-on-literature-and-elitism/>.

Colleu, Gilles. 2006. *Éditeurs indépendants: de l'âge de raison vers l'offensive*. Paris: Alliance des éditeurs indépendants.

ComLaw. 2000. Copyright Amendment (Moral Rights) Act 2000 – C2004A00752. Office of Parliamentary Counsel, Commonwealth of Australia. 21 December 2000. <http://www.comlaw.gov.au/Details/C2004A00752>.

ComLaw. 2013. Racial Discrimination Act 1975 – Section 18C – C2013C00013. Office of Parliamentary Counsel, Commonwealth of Australia. 7 January 2013. <http://www.comlaw.gov.au/Details/C2013C00013>.

Crouch, Martha L. 2001. 'From Golden Rice to Terminator Technology: Agricultural biotechnology will not feed the world or save the environment'. In Tokar, Brian (ed.). *Redesigning Life: The Worldwide Challenge to Genetic Engineering*. Melbourne: Scribe Publications; London: Zed Books; Montreal: McGill Queens University Press; Johannesburg: Witwatersrand University Press. pp. 22–39.

Daly, Mary. 1978. *Gyn/Ecology: The Meta-ethics of Radical Feminism*. Boston: Beacon Press.

Dines, Gail. 2010. *Pornland: How Porn Has Hijacked Our Sexuality*. Boston: Beacon Press; Melbourne: Spinifex Press.

Ekis Ekman, Kajsa. 2013. *Being and Being Bought: Prostitution, Surrogacy and the Split Self*. Melbourne: Spinifex Press.

Fanon, Frantz. 1973. *The Wretched of the Earth*. Translated by Constance Farrington. Harmondsworth: Penguin Books.

Fergus, Lara. 2005. 'Elsewhere in Every Country: Locating lesbian writing'. Paper presented at 9th International Interdisciplinary Congress on Women, Seoul, Korea. 21 June.

Fergus, Lara. 2010. *My Sister Chaos*. Melbourne: Spinifex Press.

Firestone, Shulamith. 1971. *The Dialectic of Sex: The Case for Feminist Revolution*. London: Paladin.

Flood, Alison. 2013. 'Coverflip: Author Maureen Johnson turns tables on gendered book covers. Novelist challenges readers to flip genders of famous book covers and expose publishers' sexist attitudes to women's fiction'. *The Guardian*. 10 May. <http://www.theguardian.com/books/2013/may/09/coverflip-maureen-johnson-gender-book>.

Frye, Marilyn. 1983. 'Oppression'. In *The Politics of Reality: Essays in Feminist Theory*. Trumansburg, NY: The Crossing Press.

Galeano, Eduardo. 1973. *Open Veins of Latin America: Five Centuries of the Pillage of a Continent*. New York: Monthly Review Press.

Goldman, Emma. 1931. *Living My Life*. New York: Alfred A. Knopf.

Gowdy, John and Carl N. McDaniel. 1995. 'One World, One Experiment: Addressing the biodiversity-economics conflict'. *Ecological Economics* 15 (3). pp. 181–192.

Graham, Dee L. R. with Edna I. Rawlings and Roberta K. Rigsby. 1994. *Loving to Survive: Sexual Terror, Men's Violence and Women's Lives*. New York: New York University Press.

Greer, Germaine. 1971. *The Female Eunuch*. London: Paladin.

Griffin, Susan. 1982. *Pornography and Silence: Culture's Revenge Against Nature*. San Francisco: HarperCollins.

Guillaumin, Colette. 1995. *Racism, Sexism, Power and Ideology*. London: Routledge.

Harrison, Dan and Jonathan Swan. 2014. 'Attorney-General George Brandis: "People do have a right to be bigots."' *Sydney Morning Herald*. 24 March. <http://www.smh.com.au/federal-politics/political-news/attorneygeneral-george-brandis-people-do-have-a-right-to-be-bigots-20140324-35dj3.html#ixzz34sUITHhp>.

Hawthorne, Susan. 1989. 'The Politics of the Exotic: The paradox of cultural voyeurism'. *Meanjin* 48 (2). pp. 259–268.

Hawthorne, Susan. 1996. 'From Theories of Indifference to a Wild Politics'. In Bell, Diane and Renate Klein (eds). *Radically Speaking: Feminism Reclaimed*. Melbourne: Spinifex Press.

Hawthorne, Susan. 2002. *Wild Politics: Feminism, Globalisation and Bio/diversity*. Melbourne: Spinifex Press.

Hawthorne, Susan. 2003a. 'The Australia–United States Free Trade Agreement'. *Arena Magazine* 63. February–March. pp. 29–32.

Hawthorne, Susan. 2003b. 'Corporate Biotechnology: Gene patents, market dynamics versus public good, biomedical marketing strategies'. Paper presented at Within and Beyond the Limits of Human Nature: Working Conference on the Challenges of the New Human Genetic Technologies. 12–15 October. Berlin.

Hawthorne, Susan. 2004. 'The Political Uses of Obscurantism: Gender mainstreaming and intersectionality'. *Development Bulletin* 89. pp. 87–91.

Hawthorne, Susan. 2005. 'GATS and Women: To what extent will women lose as the General Agreement on Trade in Services becomes embedded in the global economy?'. 9th International Interdisciplinary Congress on Women. Seoul, Korea. <https://jamescook.academia.edu/SusanHawthorne>.

Hawthorne, Susan. 2012a. 'To Whinge or Not to Whinge: Marginalising feminist writing in Australia'. *Rochford Street Review*. 22 May. <http://rochfordstreetreview.com/2012/05/22/to-whinge-or-not-to-whinge-marginalising-feminist-writing-in-australia/>.

Hawthorne, Susan. 2012b. 'Shades of Grey: What now that BDSM has gone mainstream?'. Australian Women's and Gender Studies Conference. 21 November. UNSW. <https://jamescook.academia.edu/SusanHawthorne>.

Hawthorne, Susan. 2013. *Cow*. Melbourne: Spinifex Press.

Hayden, Casey and Mary King. 1965. 'Feminism and the Civil Rights Movement'. <http://www.wwnorton.com/college/history/archive/resources/documents/ch34_02.htm>.

Herman, Judith L. 1992. 'Complex PTSD: A syndrome in survivors of prolonged and repeated trauma'. *Journal of Traumatic Stress* 5 (3). pp. 377–391.

Hynes, H. Patricia. 1999. 'Consumption: North American perspectives'. In Silliman, Jael and Ynestra Kind (eds). *Dangerous Intersections: Feminist Perspectives on Population, Environment and Development*. Cambridge, MA: South End Press.

International Alliance of Independent Publishers. 2007. *International Declaration of Independent Publishers for the Protection and Promotion of Bibliodiversity*. Paris: International Alliance of Independent Publishers.

International Alliance of Independent Publishers. 2013a. 'Book Donations: Rethinking the system'. International Assembly of Independent Publishers Workshop: Strengthening and keeping bibliodiversity alive. 20–21 March. BULAC, Paris. <http://www.alliance-editeurs.org/IMG/pdf/first_conclusions_book_donations_workshop_assembly_2013_and_2014.pdf>. Accessed 24 May 2014.

International Alliance of Independent Publishers. 2013b. 'Local and National Languages: What opportunities for publishing in Africa?'. International Assembly of Independent Publishers Workshop: Strengthening and keeping bibliodiversity alive. 11–13 June. Ouagadougou, Burkina Faso.

International Alliance of Independent Publishers. 2014a. 'Bibliodiversity'. <http://www.alliance-editeurs.org/bibliodiversity>.

International Alliance of Independent Publishers. 2014b. 'Digital Publishing: What issues for bibliodiversity in the Arabic-speaking world?'. 12 May. <http://www.alliance-editeurs.org/IMG/pdf/press_release_digital_publishing_arab_world_2_.pdf>.

Jeffreys, Sheila. 1997. *The Idea of Prostitution*. Melbourne: Spinifex Press.

Jeffs, Sandy. 2000. *Poems from the Madhouse*. Melbourne: Spinifex Press.

Jensen, Robert. 2005. *The Heart of Whiteness: Confronting Race, Racism and White Privilege*. San Francisco: City Lights.

Jensen, Robert. 2007. *Getting Off: Pornography and the End of Masculinity*. Cambridge, MA: South End Press.

Klein, Naomi. 2007. *The Shock Doctrine: The Rise of Disaster Capitalism*. Camberwell, Vic: Penguin Australia.

Kohn, Bob. 2014. 'How Book Publishers Can Beat Amazon'. *The New York Times*. 30 May. <http://www.nytimes.com/2014/05/31/opinion/how-book-publishers-can-beat-amazon.html?emc=eta1&_r=0>.

Kozlowski, Michael. 2014. 'OverDrive Acquires Cloud Based Company Booki.sh'. *Good e-Reader*. 5 March. <http://goodereader.com/blog/e-book-news/overdrive-acquires-cloud-based-company-booki-sh>.

Kulesz, Octavio. 2011. 'Digital Publishing in the Developing World'. Paris: International Alliance of Independent Publishers. <http://alliance-lab.org/etude/?lang=en>.

Lim, Kwanhui. 2011. 'What Really Went Wrong for Borders and Angus & Robertson?' *The Conversation*. 24 March. <http://theconversation.com/what-really-went-wrong-for-borders-and-angus-and-robertson-341>.

Mairs, Nancy. 1992. 'On Being a Cripple'. *Plaintext*. Tucson: University of Arizona Press. pp. 9–21.

McLellan, Betty. 2010. *Unspeakable: A Feminist Ethic of Speech*. Townsville: OtherWise Publications.

Meadows, Donella H. 2008. *Thinking in Systems*. White River Junction, VT: Chelsea Green Publishing.

Menon, Ritu. 1990. 'Coedición Simultánea de Libros Feministas'. *Debats, Debates, Dibattiti, Panel Discussions, Besprechungen*. Barcelona: IV Fira Internacional del Llibre Feminista.

Mies, Maria. 1986/1999. *Patriarchy and Accumulation on a World Scale: Women in the International Division of Labour*. London: Zed Books; Melbourne: Spinifex Press.

Mies, Maria, Veronika Bennholdt-Thomsen and Claudia von Werlhof. 1988. *Women: The Last Colony*. New Delhi: Kali for Women.

Mies, Maria and Veronika Bennholdt-Thomsen. 1999. *The Subsistence Perspective: Beyond the Globalised Economy*. London: Zed Books; Melbourne: Spinifex Press.

Morrison, Toni. 1993. *Playing in the Dark: Whiteness and Literary Imagination*. New York: Random House.

Namjoshi, Suniti. 1996. *Building Babel*. Melbourne: Spinifex Press.

Ndumbe, Prince Kum'a III. 2007. 'Stopping Intellectual Genocide in African Universities'. *Pambazuka News* 312. <http://www.pambazuka.org/>.

Nicholls, Christine. 2014. '"Dreamtime" and "The Dreaming": An introduction'. *The Conversation*. 29 January. <http://theconversation.com/dreamtime-and-the-dreaming-an-introduction-20833>.

Plath, Sylvia. 2013. *The Bell Jar*. London: Faber and Faber.

Pouliquen, Gwenael and Jacques Testard. 2010. 'Interview with André Schiffrin'. *The White Review*. October. <http://www.thewhitereview.org/interviews/interview-with-andre-schiffrin/>.

Raymond, Janice G. 1994 *Women as Wombs: Reproductive Technology and the Battle over Women's Freedom*. Melbourne: Spinifex Press.

Raymond, Janice G. 2013. *Not a Choice, Not a Job: Exposing the Myths about Prostitution and the Global Sex Trade*. Melbourne: Spinifex Press.

Robin, Marie-Monique. 2010. *The World According to Monsanto: Pollution, Politics and Power*. Melbourne: Spinifex Press; New Delhi: Tulika Books; New York: The New Press.

Roy, Arundhati. 1999. *The Cost of Living*. London: Flamingo.

Roy, Arundhati. 2003. *War Talk*. Cambridge, MA: South End Press.

Said, Edward W. 1995. *Orientalism: Western Conceptions of the Orient*. London: Penguin Books.

Schiffrin, André. 2001. *The Business of Books: How International Conglomerates Took over Publishing and Changed the Way We Read*. London: Verso.

Schmitz, Sonja. 2001. 'Cloning Profits: The revolution in agricultural technology'. In Tokar, Brian (ed.). *Redesigning Life: The Worldwide Challenge to Genetic Engineering*. Melbourne: Scribe Publications; London: Zed Books; Montreal: McGill Queens University Press; Johannesburg: Witwatersrand University Press. pp. 44–50.

Seager, Joni. 1997. *The State of Women in the World*. Harmondsworth: Penguin Books.

Shapiro, Gisèle. 2014. 'Translation as a Weapon in the Struggle Against Cultural Hegemony in the Era of Globalization'. *Bibliodiversity: Translation and Globalization* 3. February. pp. 33–42.

Shiva, Vandana. 1991. *The Violence of the Green Revolution: Third World Agriculture, Ecology and Politics*. Penang: Third World Network.

Shiva, Vandana. 1993. *Monocultures of the Mind: Perspectives on Biodiversity and Biotechnology*. Penang: Third World Network.

Shiva, Vandana. 1994. *Close to Home: Women Reconnect Ecology, Health and Development*. New Delhi: Kali for Women.

Shiva, Vandana. 2012. *Making Peace with the Earth: Beyond Resource, Land and Food Wars*. New Delhi: Women Unlimited; Melbourne: Spinifex Press.

Solanas, Valerie. 1967. *SCUM Manifesto*. New York: Olympia Press.

Soto, Mikel. 2013. 'Txalapata, Basque Country: Distribution and Promotion of Human and Social Sciences Books: What innovative strategies to succeed?'. International Alliance of Independent Publishers Workshop. 13 October. Frankfurt.

Stark, Christine and Rebecca Whisnant (eds). 2004. *Not For Sale: Feminists Resisting Prostitution and Pornography*. Melbourne: Spinifex Press.

Stoltenberg, John. 1990. *Refusing to Be a Man*. London: Fontana Collins.

Stone, Michael K. n.d. 'Ecological Principles'. Center for Ecoliteracy. <http://www.ecoliteracy.org/nature-our-teacher/ecological-principles>.

Sullivan, Mary Lucille. 2007. *Making Sex Work: A Failed Experiment with Legalised Prostitution*. Melbourne: Spinifex Press.

Swanson, Timothy. 1996. 'The Reliance of Northern Economies on Southern Biodiversity: Biodiversity as information'. *Ecological Economics* 17 (1). pp. 1–8.

Tankard Reist, Melinda and Abigail Bray (eds). 2011. *Big Porn Inc.: Exposing the Harms of the Global Pornography Industry*. Melbourne: Spinifex Press.

Thompson, John B. 2010. *Merchants of Culture: The Publishing Business in the Twenty-First Century*. Cambridge, UK: Polity.

Tuhiwai Smith, Linda. 1999. *Decolonising Methodologies: Research and Indigenous Peoples*. Otago: Otago University Press; London: Zed Books.

Wangoola, Paul. 2000. 'Mpambo, the African Multiversity: A philosophy to rekindle the African spirit'. In Dei, George J. Sefa, Budd L. Hall and Dorothy Goldin Rosenberg (eds). *Indigenous Knowledges in Global Contexts: Multiple Readings of Our World*. Toronto: OISE/UT, published in association with University of Toronto Press. pp. 265–277.

Watson, Don. 2003. *Death Sentence: The Decay of Public Language*. Sydney: Knopf.

Watson, Don. 2005. *Dictionary of Weasel Words, Contemporary Clichés, Cant and Management Jargon*. Sydney: Random House Australia.

Williams, Patricia J. 1991. *The Alchemy of Race and Rights: Diary of a Law Professor*. Cambridge, MA: Harvard University Press.

Wills, Meredith Sue. 2001. '*The Business of Books* by André Schiffrin' [Review]. American Ethical Union Library. <http://www.meredithsuewillis.com/Business%20of%20Books.html>. Accessed 22 April, 2014.

Wittig, Monique. 1976. 'The Category of Sex'. In Wittig, Monique. 1992. *The Straight Mind and Other Essays*. Boston: Beacon Press. pp. 1–8.

Wittig, Monique. 1985. 'The Mark of Gender'. In Wittig, Monique. 1992. *The Straight Mind and Other Essays*. Boston: Beacon Press.

Wittig, Monique. 1992. *The Straight Mind and Other Essays*. Boston: Beacon Press.

Woolf, Virginia. 1953/1975. *A Writer's Diary*. Edited by Leonard Woolf. London: The Hogarth Press.

Other Books from Spinifex Press

Wild Politics:
Feminism, Globalisation and Bio/diversity

Susan Hawthorne

Dominant culture knowledge diminishes the knowledge and understanding of the powerless, and because the knowledge of the powerless is regarded with contempt, the powerful are cut off from greater understanding. The powerful suffer from the syndrome of Dominant Culture Stupidities.

Looking for a new way forward, or a different explanation of what is currently happening? Susan Hawthorne challenges the universal endorsement of global Western culture with her concept of biodiversity, arguing that biodiversity is a useful metaphor for understanding social, political, and economic relations in the globalised world of the twenty-first century. She provides a visionary outlook and proposes ways forward that emphasise social justice, multiversity and an ecologically grounded feminist philosophy.

[Wild Politics] is a passionate book offering a kaleidoscope of ideas, arresting ways of seeing things, and possible solutions for many of the man-contrived environmental messes across the violated globe. Its barefaced audacity is its greatest attraction. Hawthorne has blazed a trail for others to follow.

—Alan Patience, Best Books of 2002, *Australian Book Review*

Rights: World
ISBN: 9781876756246
eBook: available

*If you would like to know more about Spinifex Press
write for a free catalogue or visit our website.*

SPINIFEX PRESS
PO Box 212 North Melbourne
Victoria 3051 Australia
www.spinifexpress.com.au